The SILVER PLATTER

simple to spectacular

WHOLESOME, FAMILY-FRIENDLY RECIPES

from the kitchen of
DANIELLA SILVER
with tips & techniques from
NORENE GILLETZ

Photography and Food Styling by EyeCandyTO
Ann Gagno *and* Abraham Wornovitzky
Art Direction by Atara Yunger

Published by **ARTSCROLL / SHAAR PRESS**
4401 Second Avenue / Brooklyn, NY 11232 / (718) 921-9000
www.artscroll.com

Distributed in Israel by **SIFRIATI / A. GITLER**
Moshav Magshimim / Israel

Distributed in Europe by **LEHMANNS**
Unit E, Viking Business Park, Rolling Mill Road
Jarrow, Tyne and Wear, NE32 3DP / England

Distributed in Australia and New Zealand by **GOLDS WORLD OF JUDAICA**
3-13 William Street / Balaclava, Melbourne 3183, Victoria / Australia

Distributed in South Africa by **KOLLEL BOOKSHOP**
Northfield Centre / 17 Northfield Avenue / Glenhazel 2192
Johannesburg, South Africa

ISBN-10: 1-4226-1557-X / ISBN-13: 978-1-4226-1557-7

Printed in Canada

Acknowledgments

To my wonderful husband, JEFFERY. Thank you for being my Number One recipe taster. Most importantly, thank you for being my backbone throughout this entire process and keeping me true to myself. This book would not have been the same without your support along the way. I love you.

To EMILY, ALISHA, and SORELLE, my 3 little girlies. I love you more than words can say. I wrote this book for you.

To my mom, RESA LITWACK. Thank you for testing recipes, dreaming up layouts, being my friend and my strength, and standing by me every step of the way. You are so creatively gifted; my book could not have been done without you.

ALAN LITWACK. Thank you for teaching me how to eat more than just chicken and for all of your guidance along the way.

To my dad, ARIEH GLUSTEIN. Thanks for your love and support, and for helping me achieve my dreams. Even after this book is published, you'd better still come by for leftovers!

To my mother-in-law, BONNY SILVER. Thank you for always giving me support and encouragement, testing recipes, and for teaching me to love and appreciate food.

To my grandparents, BUBBIE NOREEN and SABA CYRIL LAX, and BUBBIE MENA GLUSTEIN. Thank you for your love and encouragement always and for passing down your creative talents and some spectacular family recipes! A special thanks to Bubbie Noreen for helping to edit the book.

To RABBI (UNCLE MOSHE) GLUSTEIN. Thank you for being a pillar in our family. We all know we can always pick up the phone to call you. Thank you for helping me get where I am today.

To ATARA and GADI YUNGER. Atara — Thank you for all your hard work and commitment, you really came through for me. Your creative vision set the stage for my book. Gadi — Thank you for your support and always coming over for a quick cookie that turns into a full meal.

To ZVI and NAOMI GLUSTEIN. Thank you for being my social-media superstars, and for setting me up for online success. You guys are always around to help me out and happily test my food.

To SHERRI SILVER. Thanks for your constant interest and excitement in the book. I love coming over and seeing my recipes being prepared in your kitchen.

HANANEL ROMER SEGAL. Thank you for helping me see this book through to the finish line. You knew what I wanted before I did, and it was in my inbox before I even asked.

To JEREMY and TALYA SILVER. Thank you for your support and for helping me to test all my gluten-free recipes!

To MIKE and EDEN LITWACK. Thank you for your constant excitement, recipe testing, and enjoying my food. Mike — I'll bake for you anytime.

To my friends, CHAYALA BISTRICER, SARAH GAL, RIVKA GROSSMAN, EMILY HERSHTAL, PAM KUHL, RACHELI RAPP, SHOSHANA SCHACHTER, CHANTAL ULMER, DORI WEISS, ALYSSA WIESEL. Thank you for your constant support. You guys are the best.

To ELISE BRADT. Thank you for helping me edit and create beautiful intros that made my recipes sound as good as they taste.

To ABE WORNOVITZKY and ANN GAGNO. Thank you for your creative food styling, and for making my dishes look delectable on camera. Each picture tells a story, which I'll remember forever.

GEDALIAH ZLOTOWITZ. Thank you for believing in my vision, for encouraging me, and for guiding me along the way.

Thank you to my talented, devoted team at ArtScroll, who took all the ingredients and merged them together to produce this beautiful book. FELICE EISNER, my editor, carefully checked each recipe and tested many of them on the way. You gave me confidence every time you got excited about a recipe. DEVORAH BLOCH, thank you for all your hard work and for putting up with me. The book looks amazing. Thanks to JUDI DICK and TOVA OVITS for your helpful comments and fantastic proofreading. Thank you to MIRIAM PASCAL for your creative marketing skills.

ERIN TEMPLE. Thank you for the amazing work you did for the nutritional analysis.

Thank you, BETTER BATTER GLUTEN-FREE FLOUR, for providing the gluten-free flour used to test the recipes.

RYAN CAMPBELL. Thank you for enjoying my baked goods and giving honest feedback, and for teaching me how to make healthier choices for me and my family.

REYNA BELARDO. Thank you for being my sous chef. You were a second set of hands in the kitchen, and I couldn't have done it without you.

Lastly, but most importantly, to NORENE GILLETZ. You are my partner, my teacher, my editor, my friend, and after all this, a part of my family. Thank you for sharing your wisdom, strength, courage, knowledge, and insight. You believed in me and encouraged me to pursue my dreams. Thank you for helping my cookbook dream become a reality.

"Good food goes best with friends and family, and if you don't have an occasion, make one!"

Table of Contents

"I believe that you eat with your eyes first, so each dish in this cookbook was created to have aesthetic appeal. Food has to look beautiful to be appetizing."

Introduction

I absolutely love and get great satisfaction from being in the kitchen even though I'm not a professional chef nor have I gone to culinary school. I love to cook for my family and friends and look forward to any opportunity to be creative and innovative with my meals.

I belong to the "desserty" subset of foodie culture. I need something sweet after every meal. Actually, I need two or three sweet things to satisfy me. As a child, I always enjoyed cooking and baking for my family. When I was 10, I remember baking the most elaborate cheesecake for our Shavuot dinner. It was such an accomplishment, and my family was amazed! Of course, they only had a small taste because I pretty much ate the whole thing.

At 22, Jeffery Silver and I were married. We have three little girls, who are the loves of our lives. Watching them grow has only increased my desire to cook well and eat right.

My family has a long history of artistic talent. We all seem to have developed our creativity in different ways. Mine has manifested itself through food. Its presentation, the color of the ingredients, and the blending of textures are all aspects of an art form. I believe that you eat with your eyes first, so each dish in this cookbook was created to have aesthetic appeal. Food has to look beautiful to be appetizing. Then it must taste just as wonderful as it looks.

As a mother of children with allergies, it didn't take long for me to begin experimenting in the kitchen. I started creating my own original recipes because one of my daughters has a nut allergy and another is highly allergic to gluten/wheat. When I first discovered they had serious allergies, I felt overwhelmed by the task of recreating some of my favorite go-to recipes. I had to empty my pantry of many familiar, favorite ingredients and start from scratch.

Those of you who have allergies in the family know this is a great challenge. I had no idea where to begin, but with the help of family, friends, the Internet, and a little ingenuity, I was slowly able to make the necessary changes in my kitchen to accommodate my family's new diet.

They say every cloud has a "silver" lining, and necessity is the mother of invention. In eliminating certain foods from our household, I've learned to understand what's really involved in choosing the best ingredients: What's healthy, what's not; what's processed, what's not; and most importantly, what I want to serve my family to keep them satisfied, strong, and happy.

I've been working diligently on this book for two years. I've enjoyed the process more than I could have ever imagined. The highlight for me has been the opportunity to use my recipes to teach people how to cook with ingredients that suit their needs. The delicious dishes I've developed have shown my children that eating within their restrictions can be an enjoyable experience.

This cookbook has been a labor of love shared by my husband and our children. If what I've learned through my family's experience with food can help others through their own journey with food allergies, I will feel a great sense of accomplishment. That, to me, will be the success of this cookbook.

–Daniella

Crunchy Celery & Cucumber Salad, p. 68

Pistachio Biscotti, p. 272

"We hope that you enjoy this cookbook as much as we loved creating it for you and your family."

About Us ...

Intergenerational relationships are often priceless and rich, and Daniella and Norene were lucky enough to develop such a relationship.

Daniella Born into a long line of fine artists and graphic designers, I discovered my own artistic talents in the kitchen when I began experimenting with the preparation and presentation of food. I've loved to cook and bake since childhood, and, growing up, I relished creating unique dishes for my family and friends, presenting each dish in a surprising or innovative way.

Now, as a young mom, I've come to realize that my true passion lies in the culinary arts. I began to collect my recipes and ideas in a binder; the more I collected, the more new ideas I had. The idea of compiling my culinary creations into a cookbook came to mind, but despite my enthusiasm, it felt like an impossible dream, a vision that I never thought could become a reality.

After discussing the concept of a cookbook with my husband and immediate family, I decided to explore the possibilities; maybe my dream could become a reality.

I phoned Norene Gilletz, a well-known local author who had published nine successful cookbooks. Although I did not know Norene personally, I felt a close connection to her, as I am a product of Norene's *Second Helpings, Please!* Both my mother and grandmother used *Second Helpings* as a staple in their kitchens. Raised on family favorites such as Spanish Beef Rice, Sweet and Sour Meatballs, Salmon Patties, Lokshin Kugel, and Peas and Mushrooms, I was inspired to create my own menus and dishes.

My heart raced as I dialed Norene's number. I thought, "What will she say? Will she even meet with me?"

What I didn't know was that despite her hugely successful career and established expertise, Norene is a down-to-earth, friendly person who is very generous with her time and her advice. Norene gives people as much guidance as they need; each person who seeks her help is treated with patience and respect. After a wonderful and welcoming first phone call, Norene agreed to meet with me.

Walking into Norene's home for the first time was slightly intimidating, to say the least. I had no professional experience in the culinary industry, and I'd certainly never written a cookbook, but I brought along my binder full of recipes and ideas and walked in with confidence, knowing that when I put my mind to something, I always give it my all.

Norene When I first met Daniella and saw her passion and commitment, I was very excited about helping her achieve her goal of writing her own cookbook. Daniella reminded me of myself when I was her age, with her young family, very involved in community projects. Passionate to learn everything she could about food, and with a beautiful sense of color and design, Daniella had a special talent for transforming simple ingredients into spectacular dishes.

Since my children are now grown up and have their own families and we all live in different cities, I'm no longer cooking the same way on a regular basis, except for holidays and special occasions when our family gathers. Working with Daniella was an opportunity to use my culinary wisdom and knowledge in a productive way, making a difference for future generations.

Daniella It was the coming together of two generations — a match made in heaven. For the last two years, Norene and I worked together in her kitchen on my overflowing binder of loose papers. While Norene drank tea and ate yogurt, I noshed on nuts and drank hot water. We progressed to taste-testing the recipes, made tweaks, added modifications, and included helpful tips to make each one the best it could be. Before long, we became close friends and spoke several times a day, sharing ideas. Even on holidays and many Shabbats, Norene would happily join our family table.

We quickly realized the tremendous impact that we could have as a culinary team. We recognized our strengths and weaknesses and saw that we had something unique. We realized the benefit of merging our special gifts. I brought a unique talent for developing creative, innovative recipes for today's generation, and Norene brought a wealth of culinary knowledge and expertise. We saw that the purpose of writing this cookbook is to share the wisdom from one generation to the next and to carry traditions forward in a creative new way.

The Silver Platter is a labor of love, blending health and food trends with traditional kosher recipes, meeting the needs of today's modern family.

Daniella & Norene

Banana Chocolate Chip Cake, p. 294

Appetizers

For nutritional information on this section, see pages 319–320

Rice rolls are also known as fresh spring rolls. They are the perfect appetizer for an Asian-inspired meal. I slice the rolls in half so my kids can dip them easily — dipping is the best part!

Asian-Style Rice Paper Rolls

pareve | gluten-free | do not freeze | yields 8-10 servings

Ingredients

2 ripe avocados, halved, pitted, and thinly sliced

1 mango, peeled, pitted, and cut into matchsticks

4 baby cucumbers, cut into matchsticks (do not peel)

½ small red onion, thinly sliced

2 cups baby spinach leaves

8-10 large rice paper wrappers (about 8 inches in diameter)

Dipping Sauce

⅓ cup soy sauce or tamari

1 tsp toasted sesame oil

2 cloves garlic, minced (about 1 tsp)

1 tsp minced fresh ginger

1 scallion, thinly sliced

Method

1. Line a large tray with parchment paper; set aside. Place avocados, mango, cucumbers, red onion, and spinach into separate bowls.

2. Fill a pie plate with lukewarm water. Working with one rice paper at a time, immerse it in water for about 5-7 seconds or until pliable. (Be careful, as they tear easily.) Place onto a clean towel; pat dry.

3. Layer a small amount each of avocado, mango, cucumber, onion, and spinach on each wrapper, leaving a 1-inch border on all sides. Do not overfill. Lift bottom edge of wrapper over filling, then fold in sides and roll up tightly. Place seam side down on prepared tray.

4. Repeat with remaining wrappers and filling; leave about a half-inch between rolls as you place them on the tray, so they don't stick to each other. Cover with damp paper towels and refrigerate until serving time.

5. **Dipping Sauce:** In a small bowl, stir together dipping sauce ingredients.

6. To serve, slice each roll in half on the diagonal and place on individual plates or a serving platter. Serve with dipping sauce.

Norene's Notes

- All the fillings and the dipping sauce can be prepared the night before; sprinkle the avocado with lemon juice to prevent discoloration. Cover tightly with plastic wrap and refrigerate. Rice rolls can be filled and assembled up to 4 hours before serving time.
- To keep your recipes gluten-free, use gluten-free soy sauce or tamari.

There is something mysterious about mushrooms, with their rich and earthy taste. When seasoned and sautéed with a few simple ingredients, they become infused with flavor, yet remain silky and luscious.

Honey-Garlic Mushrooms & Rice

pareve | gluten-free | do not freeze | yields 6 servings

Ingredients

Rice

2 cups water

1 cup basmati rice, rinsed and drained

3 Tbsp seasoned rice vinegar

1-2 Tbsp extra virgin olive oil

kosher salt

freshly ground black pepper

Mushrooms

2 Tbsp grapeseed or olive oil

2 lb/1 kg assorted mushrooms, sliced (8-10 cups)

2 Tbsp honey

3 Tbsp soy sauce or tamari

1 Tbsp seasoned rice vinegar

3 cloves garlic, minced (about 1½ tsp)

½ tsp dried thyme

fresh chives, chopped, for garnish

Method

1. **Rice:** Bring water to a boil in a medium saucepan over high heat. Add rice, cover, and simmer for 20 minutes. Remove from heat and let stand, covered, for 10 minutes. Fluff with a fork. Stir in rice vinegar, oil, salt, and pepper; mix well. Adjust seasonings to taste. Set aside.

2. **Mushrooms:** Meanwhile, heat oil in a large wok over medium-high heat. Add mushrooms and sauté, stirring often, for 10-12 minutes, or until golden and liquid has evaporated. If liquid is left in the pan after sautéing, just drain it off.

3. Stir honey, soy sauce, vinegar, garlic, and thyme into the mushrooms.

4. **Assembly:** Plate a mound of hot rice for each serving. Spoon on hot mushroom mixture. Garnish with chives.

Norene's Notes

• Instead of basmati rice, use a rice blend (e.g., white and brown basmati); follow cooking directions on the package. Black rice or red quinoa makes a dramatic presentation.

• Having vegetarians as guests? Serve this as a main course using quinoa to make a complete meal. Yields 4 main-dish servings.

No one can resist these baked, guilt-free egg rolls. Packed with Asian-style veggies and served with a dollop of dipping sauce, guests will be lingering around the appetizer table hoping for a second batch to arrive.

Baked Vegetable Egg Rolls

pareve | freezes well | yields 16-18 egg rolls

Ingredients

2 Tbsp vegetable oil

2 bags (16 oz/454 g each) shredded cabbage

1 cup grated carrots

1 red bell pepper, halved and thinly sliced

4 scallions, thinly sliced

3 cloves garlic, minced (about 1½ tsp)

3 Tbsp rice vinegar

3 Tbsp soy sauce or tamari

pinch chili flakes (optional)

1 pkg egg roll wrappers

additional oil, for brushing

Dipping Sauce

¼ **cup** soy sauce or tamari

¼ **cup** rice vinegar

2 Tbsp honey

1 tsp toasted sesame oil

pinch chili flakes

Method

1. Heat oil in a large wok over high heat. Add cabbage, carrots, peppers, and scallions. Stir-fry for 5 minutes, until tender-crisp.

2. Stir in garlic, rice vinegar, soy sauce, and chili flakes, if using; cook 2-3 minutes. Let cool. Drain well.

3. Preheat oven to 425°F. Line a rimmed baking sheet with aluminum foil; coat with nonstick cooking spray.

4. Place a spoonful of veggies onto an egg roll wrapper, leaving a 1-inch border on all sides. Do not overfill. Lift bottom edge of wrapper over filling, then fold in sides and roll up tightly. Place seam side down on prepared baking sheet.

5. Repeat with remaining wrappers and filling, leaving about half an inch between rolls so they don't stick to each other.

6. Brush tops lightly with oil.

7. Bake, uncovered, for 10-15 minutes, until golden brown.

8. **Dipping sauce:** Combine sauce ingredients in a small bowl. Serve with egg rolls.

Norene's Notes

• Filling ingredients must be drained and cooled before rolling or egg rolls will become soggy.

• To prevent edges from drying out, cover filled wrappers with a damp paper towel while filling the remaining egg rolls.

These patties are a hit with adults and kids alike. The silky texture of salmon lends itself perfectly to this preparation, resulting in golden bites of goodness. I also make these for dinner quite often and serve them with various salads.

Fresh Salmon Patties

pareve | passover option | gluten-free option | freezes well | yields 12-15 patties

Ingredients

1 stalk celery, cut into chunks

1 cup baby spinach

½ small red onion

1 lb/500 g ground salmon

1 cup bread crumbs (gluten-free or regular)

2 eggs

4-6 drops hot sauce

1 Tbsp fresh lemon juice

1 tsp kosher salt

¼ tsp black pepper

2 Tbsp grapeseed oil, plus more if needed

Method

1. Preheat oven to 400°F. Line a baking sheet with parchment paper.

2. In a food processor fitted with the steel blade, combine celery, spinach, and onion. Process with very quick on/off pulses, until coarsely chopped.

3. Add salmon, crumbs, eggs, hot sauce, lemon juice, salt, and pepper. Process with 3-4 quick on/off pulses, just until combined, scraping down sides of bowl with a rubber spatula if necessary. Do not overprocess!

4. Form mixture into 2-inch balls and place in a single layer on prepared baking sheet. Flatten each ball to half-inch thickness by pressing down gently with the palm of your hand. (See Norene's Notes, below.)

5. Heat oil in a nonstick skillet over medium-high heat. Working in batches, fry salmon patties for 4-5 minutes per side, or until nicely browned.

6. Place salmon patties onto baking sheet lined with clean parchment paper. Bake, uncovered, for 8-10 minutes or until cooked through.

Norene's Notes

- Here's another easy way to flatten the patties: Place a second sheet of parchment paper on top of salmon balls. Cover with another baking sheet and press gently, flattening patties. Pantastic!

- If you can't find fresh ground salmon, cut skinless boneless salmon fillets into chunks. Process with several on/off pulses, just until minced.

- Passover Option: Use crushed Passover crackers instead of bread crumbs. Omit hot sauce; substitute with ½ tsp sweet paprika.

Nothing taps into today's food trends more than lightly roasted asparagus topped with a soft-poached egg. This beautiful green-and-gold dish is lovely for fancy breakfasts, family brunches, or show-stopping appetizers.

Roasted Asparagus
with poached eggs

pareve | passover option | gluten-free | do not freeze | yields 4 servings

Ingredients

1 bunch asparagus (about 1 lb/500 g)

1 Tbsp olive oil

kosher salt

freshly ground black pepper

½ cup balsamic vinegar

1 tsp white vinegar

4 large eggs

Method

1. Preheat oven to 400°F. Line a baking sheet with parchment paper.

2. Bend asparagus stalks, snapping off and discarding tough ends where they break off naturally. Spread asparagus in a single layer on prepared baking sheet. Drizzle with olive oil; season with salt and pepper.

3. Roast, uncovered, for 10-12 minutes, or until asparagus is tender-crisp.

4. **Glaze:** Pour balsamic vinegar into a small saucepan. Bring to a boil; reduce heat and simmer until thick and syrupy and it has reduced by half.

5. Meanwhile, heat water in a shallow saucepan just until simmering. Stir in white vinegar and a pinch of salt.

6. Crack eggs, one at a time, into a small cup. Place the cup near the surface of the simmering water and gently slide each egg into the water. Using a slotted spoon, push the egg whites closer to the yolks so they can hold their shape. Turn off heat and cover pan. Let sit for 4 minutes, until whites are cooked.

7. **Assembly:** Divide asparagus among individual serving plates. Top each serving with a poached egg. Drizzle with balsamic glaze.

Norene's Notes

• Vinegar helps poached eggs keep their shape. For best results, be sure to use fresh eggs. Use a slotted spoon to remove eggs from the saucepan.

• Passover Option: Use Passover vinegar or lemon juice in the dressing.

Simple yet sophisticated, these beautiful eggplant fans are always a dinner party hit. Serve as an appetizer or a side dish, and garnish with fresh, roughly chopped parsley.

Baby Eggplant Fans

pareve | gluten-free | do not freeze | yields 8 servings

Ingredients

4 small baby eggplants
(about 1 lb/500 g total weight)

⅓ cup soy sauce or tamari

3 Tbsp olive oil

3 Tbsp rice vinegar

2 cloves garlic, minced
(about 1 tsp)

2 cups hummus
(store-bought or
homemade, p. 24)

¼ cup chopped fresh parsley

Method

1. Cut each eggplant in half lengthwise. Place each half, cut side down, on a cutting board and cut vertically into segments ¼-inch apart, down to but not through the stem. Make sure that segments are still attached at stem end.

2. In a large resealable bag, combine soy sauce, oil, vinegar, and garlic. Add eggplant halves; marinate for 20 minutes.

3. Preheat oven to 400°F. Line a baking sheet with parchment paper.

4. Transfer eggplants to prepared baking sheet. Discard marinade. Gently spread strips apart, forming each eggplant into a fan shape.

5. Bake, uncovered, for 25-30 minutes, or until eggplants are tender.

6. Spread ¼ cup hummus on each individual plate; top with an eggplant fan. Garnish with parsley. Alternatively, spread 2 cups hummus over a large serving platter. Top with eggplant fans; garnish with parsley.

Norene's Notes

- Eggplants come in a variety of sizes and colors, including purple, white, and striped.
- Smaller eggplants are more tender and have fewer seeds.

The hummus takes minutes to prepare; perfect with crackers, bread, or crudités, it makes an elegant individual appetizer served in parfait glasses. Fresh guacamole packs a healthy celery crunch, putting a fresh spin on a classic party favorite. Serve with tortillas or rice crackers. Hummus and guacamole can be frozen.

Spicy Lemon Hummus

pareve | gluten-free | yields about 2 cups

Ingredients

1 can (19 oz/540 ml) chickpeas, rinsed and drained

2 cloves garlic

¼ cup extra virgin olive oil

juice of **1** lemon (about 3-4 Tbsp)

2-3 Tbsp tahini (sesame paste)

½ tsp chili flakes (or to taste)

kosher salt

freshly ground black pepper

2-3 Tbsp water (optional)

Method

1. Using a food processor fitted with the steel blade, process chickpeas, garlic, oil, lemon juice, tahini, chili flakes, salt, and pepper until very smooth, about 2 minutes. Scrape down sides of bowl as needed. For a creamier texture, drizzle in 2-3 Tbsp water and process a few seconds longer. Adjust seasonings to taste.

2. Spoon into a serving bowl, cover, and refrigerate. May be stored about 1 week in the refrigerator in a tightly sealed container.

3. See Norene's Notes, below, for a delicious red pepper variation.

Norene's Notes

- Variation: For Red Pepper Hummus, add ½ cup roasted red peppers (homemade or store-bought) in step 1. Omit chili flakes.

Crunchy Guacamole

pareve | passover | gluten-free | yields about 2 cups

Ingredients

2 ripe avocados, halved and pitted

6 grape tomatoes, quartered, or **1** medium tomato, diced

1 stalk celery, diced

¼ cup diced red onion

juice of **½** lemon (about 2 Tbsp)

2 cloves garlic, minced (about 1 tsp)

kosher salt

freshly ground black pepper

Method

1. In a medium bowl, mash avocado flesh until smooth. (A potato masher does a good job.)

2. Add tomato, celery, red onion, lemon juice, garlic, salt, and pepper. Mix well.

3. Transfer to a serving bowl; press plastic wrap directly against surface. (This helps prevent discoloration.) Refrigerate until serving time. Use within 1-2 days.

Norene's Notes

- Extra ripe avocados? Use a food processor to process the avocado flesh and a drizzle of lemon juice until puréed. Transfer to a resealable freezer bag. Press out air, seal tightly, and freeze. When needed, thaw in the refrigerator. Drain if necessary.

Savory and smooth, this eggplant dip brings a depth of flavor to every bite, thanks to the caramelized sugars in the roasted vegetables. Perfect for impressing guests at your next get-together.

Roasted Eggplant Dip

pareve | passover | gluten-free | freezes well | yields about 2½ cups

Ingredients

1 medium eggplant
(about 1½ lb/750 g),
cut into chunks (do not peel)

1 small red onion, cut into chunks

1 bell pepper (red, yellow, or
orange), cut into chunks

3 cloves garlic

2 Tbsp extra virgin olive oil

kosher salt

freshly ground black pepper

1 tsp dried basil

2 Tbsp tomato paste

Method

1. Preheat oven to 400°F. Line a baking sheet with parchment paper.

2. In a large bowl, toss together eggplant, red onion, bell pepper, garlic, oil, salt, pepper, and basil.

3. Spread evenly on prepared baking sheet. Roast, uncovered, for 35-40 minutes, or until somewhat charred, stirring occasionally. Let cool.

4. Using a food processor fitted with the steel blade, process roasted vegetables with tomato paste until smooth. Adjust seasonings to taste.

5. Spoon into a serving bowl, cover, and refrigerate until serving time.

Norene's Notes

- You can use up the remaining tomato paste in the can by making this Quick Pizza Sauce: Combine ½ cup tomato paste, 1 cup water, and ½ tsp each garlic powder, dried basil, and oregano. Mix well.
- Passover Option: Serve with matzo or Passover crackers.

Never underestimate the innate human love for all things crunchy. There's something about that "chomp chomp" we just love to hear. Although these toasted treats do not freeze well, they will satisfy your crunchy cravings while keeping your snack habit healthy and nutritious.

Spicy Chickpeas

pareve | gluten-free | yields about 1¼ cups

Ingredients

1 can (19 oz/540 ml) chickpeas, rinsed, drained, and patted dry

1 Tbsp olive oil

1 tsp kosher salt

¼ tsp black pepper

½ tsp garlic powder

½ tsp cayenne

Method

1. Preheat oven to 400°F. Line a rimmed baking sheet with parchment paper.

2. In a large bowl, combine chickpeas, olive oil, salt, pepper, garlic powder, and cayenne. Stir well.

3. Spread chickpeas in a single layer on prepared baking sheet. Bake, uncovered, for 35-45 minutes, until golden and crunchy. Stir occasionally.

4. When cool, store in an airtight container at room temperature.

Norene's Notes

• For an Asian flavor, drizzle chickpeas with tamari instead of oil; omit salt.

Garlic-Roasted Lentils

pareve | gluten-free | yields about 2 cups

Ingredients

1 cup dried lentils (brown or green)

3 cups water

1 Tbsp olive oil

1 tsp kosher salt

¼ tsp black pepper

1 tsp garlic powder

Method

1. Rinse lentils; drain well. Place lentils and water into a saucepan; bring to a boil. Reduce heat, cover, and simmer until almost tender, 25-30 minutes. Drain well. Return lentils to pan; let cool.

2. Preheat oven to 400°F. Line a rimmed baking sheet with parchment paper.

3. Add olive oil, salt, pepper, and garlic powder to lentils. Stir well. Spread in a single layer on prepared baking sheet. Roast, uncovered, for 35-45 minutes, stirring every 10-15 minutes, until crunchy.

4. When cool, store in an airtight container at room temperature.

Norene's Notes

• If your water is very hard, use bottled water. Do not use red lentils; they will become soft and mushy.

Roasted Edamame Beans

pareve | gluten-free | yields about 2 cups

Ingredients

1 pkg (16 oz/500 g) frozen shelled edamame beans, thawed and patted dry

1 Tbsp olive oil

1 tsp kosher salt

freshly ground black pepper

Method

1. Preheat oven to 400°F. Line a rimmed baking sheet with parchment paper.

2. In a large bowl, toss edamame beans with olive oil, salt, and pepper.

3. Spread beans in a single layer on prepared baking sheet. Roast, uncovered, for 35-45 minutes, until golden-brown and crunchy. Stir occasionally.

4. When cool, store in an airtight container at room temperature.

Roasted Corn Niblets

pareve | gluten-free | yields about 1½ cups

Ingredients

2 cans (12 oz/340 g each) corn niblets, drained and patted dry

1 Tbsp olive oil

1 Tbsp sweet paprika

1 tsp kosher salt

Method

1. Preheat oven to 400°F. Line a rimmed baking sheet with parchment paper.

2. In a medium bowl, combine corn niblets with olive oil, paprika, and salt. Stir well.

3. Spread in a single layer on prepared baking sheet. Bake, uncovered, for 45-50 minutes, until browned and crunchy. Stir occasionally.

4. When cool, store in an airtight container at room temperature.

Garlic-Roasted Lentils

Roasted Corn Niblets

Spicy Chickpeas

Roasted Edamame Beans

Why mini? Because they're adorable that way! If you're short on time, skip the cute presentation and make them a bit bigger. Simmered in a savory tomato-based sauce, they're just as juicy and flavorful either way.

Mini Meatballs

meat | passover | gluten-free | freezes well | yields 8-10 servings

Ingredients

Meatballs

2 lb lean ground beef (or veal or chicken)

¼ cup minced red onion

2 cloves garlic, minced (about 1 tsp)

1 tsp dried basil

1 tsp dried parsley

1 tsp kosher salt

freshly ground black pepper

Sauce

2 cans (28 oz/796 ml each) diced or whole tomatoes, with their liquid

⅓ cup brown sugar

2 Tbsp lemon juice

4 cloves garlic, minced (about 2 tsp)

2 tsp dried basil

2 tsp dried parsley

2 bay leaves

kosher salt

freshly ground black pepper

Method

1. In a large bowl, combine ground beef, onion, garlic, basil, parsley, salt, and pepper. Mix lightly. Do not overmix or meatballs will be tough.

2. **Sauce:** In a large pot, combine tomatoes with their liquid, brown sugar, lemon juice, garlic, basil, parsley, bay leaves, salt, and pepper. Stir well. Heat until simmering, stirring occasionally.

3. Using a melon baller, shape meat into tiny balls. Add meatballs to sauce and simmer, partially covered, for 1 hour. Do not stir or meatballs will break apart.

4. Discard bay leaves. Serve meatballs on individual plates.

Norene's Notes

• No melon baller? Shape meatballs by hand, wetting your hands for easier handling.

• An easy way to stir meatballs while cooking without actually stirring is to shake the pot gently back and forth.

If you have a large group of sports-loving guys in your family, like I do, then you'd better have a few chicken wing recipes up your sleeve! These are my three top hits. With spicy, sweet, and savory options, everyone will be happy. They even freeze well!

Sweet & Spicy BBQ Wings

meat | gluten-free | yields 8 servings

Ingredients

2 dozen chicken wings (about 3 lb/1.4 kg)

kosher salt

freshly ground black pepper

½ **cup** barbecue sauce

½ **cup** brown sugar

¼ **cup** honey

1 tsp hot sauce (or to taste)

4 cloves garlic, minced (about 2 tsp)

sesame seeds, for sprinkling

Method

1. Preheat oven to 400°F. Line a baking sheet with foil; coat with nonstick cooking spray. Use tweezers to remove pinfeathers.

2. Arrange wings in a single layer on prepared baking sheet. Sprinkle with salt and pepper.

3. Bake, uncovered, for 40-45 minutes, until golden and crunchy and juices run clear. Discard accumulated fat.

4. Meanwhile, in a small saucepan, combine barbecue sauce, brown sugar, honey, hot sauce, and garlic. Heat over medium heat until bubbling, stirring occasionally. Let simmer for 2 minutes.

5. Place chicken wings into a large bowl. Toss with sauce, coating well. Sprinkle with sesame seeds to garnish.

Herbed Balsamic Wings

meat | passover | gluten-free | yields 8 servings

Ingredients

2 dozen chicken wings (about 3 lb/1.4 kg)

kosher salt

freshly ground black pepper

½ **cup** balsamic vinegar

¼ **cup** chopped fresh basil or **1 Tbsp** dried

¼ **cup** chopped fresh parsley or **1 Tbsp** dried

2 tsp fresh thyme leaves or ½ **tsp** dried

2 Tbsp honey

fresh basil leaves or parsley, for garnish

Method

1. Preheat oven to 400°F. Line a baking sheet with foil; coat with nonstick cooking spray. Use tweezers to remove pinfeathers.

2. Arrange wings in a single layer on prepared baking sheet. Sprinkle with salt and pepper.

3. Bake, uncovered, for 40-45 minutes, until golden and crunchy and juices run clear. Discard accumulated fat.

4. Meanwhile, in a small saucepan, combine balsamic vinegar, basil, parsley, thyme, and honey. Heat over medium heat until bubbling, stirring occasionally. Let simmer for 2 minutes.

5. Place chicken wings into a large bowl. Toss with sauce, coating well. Garnish with basil or parsley.

Honey-Glazed Wings

meat | gluten-free | yields 8 servings

Ingredients

2 dozen chicken wings (about 3 lb/1.4 kg)

kosher salt

freshly ground black pepper

½ cup ketchup

½ cup honey

¼ cup soy sauce or tamari

2 Tbsp lime or lemon juice

3 cloves garlic, minced (about 1½ tsp)

thinly sliced scallions, for garnish

Method

1. Preheat oven to 400°F. Line a baking sheet with foil; coat with nonstick cooking spray. Use tweezers to remove pinfeathers.

2. Arrange wings in a single layer on prepared baking sheet. Sprinkle with salt and pepper.

3. Bake, uncovered, for 40-45 minutes, until golden and crunchy and juices run clear. Discard accumulated fat.

4. Meanwhile, in a small saucepan, combine ketchup, honey, soy sauce, lime juice, and garlic. Heat over medium heat until bubbling, stirring occasionally. Let simmer for 2 minutes.

5. Place chicken wings into a large bowl. Toss with sauce, coating well. Sprinkle with scallions to garnish.

Norene's Notes

- To remove pinfeathers easily, place chicken wings into a colander. Pour boiling water over wings; drain well. Remove pinfeathers with tweezers.

- Chicken Fingers: Replace the chicken wings with 1½ lb/750 g boneless skinless chicken breasts, cut into long narrow strips. Bake, uncovered, at 400°F for 12-15 minutes, until juices run clear. Toss with sauce.

This easy-to-prepare Israeli spice rub is delicious on juicy grilled chicken or beef. These yummy three-bite samplers are best served with a lemony-garlic tahini sauce to double up on flavor. Great as an appetizer or an entrée.

Israeli-Style Satay
with tahini dipping sauce

meat | gluten-free | satay freezes well; do not freeze sauce | yields 6-8 servings

Ingredients

6 single boneless skinless chicken breasts or
1½ lb/750 g London broil

1½ tsp kosher salt

¼ tsp black pepper

3 tsp sweet paprika

3 tsp garlic powder

3 tsp onion powder

½-1 tsp cumin

¼ cup chopped fresh parsley

Special Equipment

12-16 bamboo skewers

Tahini Sauce

½ cup tahini (sesame paste)

¾ cup water

1 clove garlic, minced (about ½ tsp)

2 Tbsp lemon juice (preferably fresh)

kosher salt, to taste

Method

1. Cut chicken or London broil into long, thin strips.

2. In a medium bowl, combine salt, pepper, paprika, garlic powder, onion powder, cumin, and parsley. Mix well.

3. Add chicken strips to spices and mix well. Let stand for 30 minutes at room temperature. Meanwhile, soak bamboo skewers in water for 30 minutes.

4. Thread chicken or meat strips onto skewers.

5. Preheat grill, setting it to medium-high.

6. Grill over indirect heat for 4-5 minutes per side, until grill marks appear and juices run clear.

7. **Tahini Sauce:** Add tahini sauce ingredients to a serving bowl; stir well to combine.

8. Transfer skewers to individual plates or a serving platter and serve with tahini sauce.

Norene's Notes

- No grill? Sauté the chicken strips in a nonstick skillet for 4-5 minutes per side, or bake it, uncovered, at 400°F for 12-15 minutes.
- Tahini is usually found in Middle Eastern stores. It is made from ground sesame seeds and makes a great addition to hummus.
- To prevent it from becoming rancid, store tahini in the refrigerator once the container has been opened.
- This tahini sauce keeps about 2 weeks in the refrigerator.

This delicious homemade treat is really so easy to make. Not only does this beef come out of the oven crispy and chewy, it has a depth of flavor that is truly amazing.

Crunchy Corned Beef Strips

meat | gluten-free | do not freeze | yields 6 servings

Ingredients

1 lb/500 g deli corned beef, thinly sliced

¼ cup ketchup

3 Tbsp honey

2 Tbsp soy or tamari sauce

Method

1. Preheat broiler. Coat a perforated baking sheet or ovenproof grid with nonstick cooking spray. Place onto a foil-lined baking sheet.

2. In a small bowl, stir together ketchup, honey, and soy sauce to make a glaze.

3. Arrange corned beef slices in a single layer on prepared baking sheet or grid. Brush both sides of each slice with glaze.

4. Broil for 3-5 minutes, or until golden and crispy. Let cool.

5. Store in an airtight container in the refrigerator. Will remain fresh for 4-5 days.

Norene's Notes

- Deli meats contain nitrites and nitrates, and they are high in sodium, so save them for an occasional treat.
- Always accompany deli with a food that's rich in vitamin C, such as tomatoes, or serve oranges or melons for dessert. This helps reduce the formation of harmful toxins.

Soups

For nutritional information on this section, see pages 320–321

When cold winds started to blow, this hearty cabbage soup was one of the staple dishes of my mom, Resa Litwack. With the warm, traditional flavors of carrots, potatoes, and celery, this soup is a no-fail classic.

Mom's Cabbage Soup

pareve | meat option | passover | gluten-free | freezes well | yields 10 servings

Ingredients

2 Tbsp olive oil

2 large onions, sliced

4 cloves garlic, minced (about 2 tsp)

1 large cabbage, cored and sliced (see Norene's Notes, below)

4 stalks celery, sliced

3 carrots, peeled and sliced

2 potatoes, peeled and diced

2 cans (28 oz/796 ml each) diced or whole tomatoes, with their liquid

6 cups water or vegetable broth

1 Tbsp kosher salt

freshly ground black pepper

2 tsp dried basil

1 tsp dried oregano

Method

1. Heat oil in a large soup pot over medium heat. Add onions and garlic; sauté for 6-8 minutes, or until golden.

2. Stir in cabbage, celery, carrots, potatoes, tomatoes with their liquid, and water. Add salt, pepper, basil, and oregano; bring to a boil.

3. Reduce heat. Simmer, partially covered, for 1½ hours, stirring occasionally. Adjust seasonings to taste.

Norene's Notes

- Short on time? Instead of slicing up a whole cabbage, use 2 pkgs (16 oz/500 g each) coleslaw mix or shredded white cabbage.
- Sweet and Sour Variation: Add ⅓-½ cup brown sugar and 2 Tbsp lemon juice.
- Meat Variation: Add 2 lb flanken (short ribs) in step 2. Once soup comes to a boil, skim well. Increase cooking time to 2½ hours.

This super-healthy soup is low in fat, packed with nutrients, and incorporates natural soothers like ginger, cinnamon, and lemon. The ginger and garlic add a subtle spiciness, and the lemon zest adds a zing.

Carrot-Ginger Soup

pareve | passover | gluten-free | freezes well | yields 8 servings

Ingredients

2 Tbsp olive oil

2 onions, diced

1-2 cloves garlic, minced (about 1 tsp)

2 tsp minced fresh ginger

2 lb/1 kg carrots, peeled and chopped (about 6 cups)

4-5 cups water or vegetable broth

1 cup orange juice

1 tsp ground cinnamon

2 tsp kosher salt

freshly ground black pepper

1-2 tsp lemon juice (preferably fresh)

grated lemon zest, for garnish

Method

1. Heat oil in a large soup pot over medium heat. Add onions, garlic, and ginger; sauté for 5 minutes or until softened.

2. Stir in carrots, water, orange juice, cinnamon, salt, and pepper. Bring to a boil.

3. Reduce heat; simmer, partially covered, for 35-45 minutes, until carrots are tender. Stir occasionally.

4. Remove from heat. Add lemon juice and cool slightly.

5. Using an immersion blender, process soup until smooth. If too thick, add a little water or broth. Adjust seasonings to taste. Garnish with lemon zest.

Norene's Notes

- Variation: Use a combination of butternut squash and carrots. Add a drizzle of honey just before puréeing the soup.
- An easy way to peel fresh ginger is to scrape away the peel with the tip of a spoon.
- Ginger is an anti-inflammatory and also helps with symptoms of nausea.
- A slice of ginger the size of a quarter yields 1 tablespoon minced.

Chicken soup is a Friday-night staple in our house. Tender pieces of chicken simmer in a mix of carrots, parsnips, onions, and fresh dill, creating a delicate yet heartwarming broth — it's comfort food in a bowl.

Chicken Soup
with rice noodles

meat | passover option | gluten-free | yields 8-10 servings

Ingredients

6 single skinless boneless chicken breasts

10 cups water

1 Tbsp kosher salt

1 tsp black pepper

4 medium onions, peeled

5 carrots, peeled and cut in chunks

5 stalks celery, trimmed and cut in chunks

4 parsnips, peeled and cut in chunks

1 bunch fresh dill

1 pkg (10 oz/300 g) thin rice noodles

Method

1. Place chicken into a large pot; add water, salt, and pepper. Bring to a boil over high heat. With a slotted spoon, skim off and discard any scum that rises to the surface of the soup.

2. Add onions, carrots, celery, and parsnips. Reduce heat; simmer, partially covered, for 1 hour. Add dill; simmer 10 minutes longer. Adjust seasonings. Shred chicken or cut it into small pieces; return to pot.

3. Cook rice noodles according to package directions. Drain well. (If not using them immediately, cover with cold water and set aside.)

4. Add a portion of noodles to each soup bowl; add soup with chicken and vegetables.

Norene's Notes

- A soup pot with a pasta insert is wonderful for cooking chicken soup. There is no need to strain the soup after cooking. Just lift and separate!
- Don't cook the noodles in the soup or they will absorb too much of the broth; they will also make the soup cloudy.
- Passover Option: Omit rice noodles. Serve with spaghetti squash noodles (see p. 56).

Enjoy these four chilled and refreshing summer soups. Each is also perfect as a light dessert or paired with a piece of cake.

Strawberry-Rhubarb Soup

pareve | dairy option | passover | gluten-free | yields 6 servings

Ingredients

4 cups fresh or frozen strawberries

4 cups fresh or frozen rhubarb pieces

2 large apples, peeled, cored, and sliced

¾ cup sugar

4 cups water

6 sprigs fresh mint, for garnish

Method

1. In a medium saucepan, combine strawberries (trimmed if fresh), rhubarb, apples, sugar, and water. Bring to a boil.

2. Reduce heat. Simmer, partially covered, for 10-15 minutes or until fruit is tender. Let cool slightly.

3. Using an immersion blender, purée soup. If too thick, add a little water.

4. Transfer to a container. Cover and refrigerate for 3-4 hours or overnight.

5. Serve chilled. Garnish with fresh mint.

Norene's Notes

• Variation: For a dairy option, top with a dollop of Greek yogurt.

Watermelon Fruit Soup

pareve | passover | gluten-free | yields 6 servings

Ingredients

8 cups seedless watermelon chunks

2 Tbsp lemon juice (preferably fresh)

2 Tbsp fresh basil or mint

3 Tbsp honey

additional fresh basil or mint, for garnish

Method

1. In a food processor fitted with the steel blade, process watermelon, lemon juice, basil, and honey until puréed. (You may need to do this in batches.)

2. Transfer to a container. Cover and refrigerate for 3-4 hours or overnight.

3. Stir well. Serve chilled. Garnish with basil or mint.

Serve in martini or shot glasses for a stylish look. All but the Watermelon Fruit Soup freeze well.

Berry-Plum Soup

pareve | passover | gluten-free | yields 6-8 servings

Ingredients

12 red plums, pitted, peeled, and cut into chunks

2 cups sweet white wine

2 Tbsp honey (or to taste)

1 cinnamon stick

3 cups fresh or frozen berries

additional thinly sliced plums, for garnish

Method

1. In a medium saucepan, combine plums, wine, honey, and cinnamon stick. Bring to a boil.

2. Reduce heat. Simmer, partially covered, for 20 minutes or until plums are tender.

3. Stir in berries and simmer 5 minutes longer. Discard cinnamon stick. Cool slightly.

4. Using an immersion blender, purée soup until smooth.

5. Transfer to a container. Cover and refrigerate for 3-4 hours or overnight.

6. Serve chilled. Garnish with plum slices.

Dairy Blueberry Soup

dairy | passover | gluten-free | yields 6 servings

Ingredients

4 cups fresh or frozen blueberries, plus more for garnishing

1½ cups water

½ cup orange juice

⅓ cup honey

2 cups vanilla yogurt, plus more for garnishing

Method

1. In a medium saucepan, combine 4 cups blueberries, water, orange juice, and honey. Bring to a boil.

2. Reduce heat. Simmer, partially covered, for 5 minutes or until most of the blueberries have burst. Let cool.

3. Add yogurt and purée with an immersion blender until fairly smooth.

4. Transfer to a container. Cover and refrigerate for 3-4 hours or overnight.

5. Serve chilled. Top each serving with additional yogurt, swirling it decoratively into soup. Garnish with additional blueberries.

This Japanese-style Asian Soba Noodle Soup is high in fiber, low calorie, glycemic friendly, and gluten free. Don't freeze this soup.

Be sure not to overcook the greens in this Green Soup Bowl; when they lose that bright color, they also lose nutrients. This soup freezes well.

Asian Soba Noodle Soup

meat | gluten-free | yields 8 servings

Ingredients

1 pkg (10 oz/300 g) soba noodles

6 cups chicken or vegetable broth

½ cup rice vinegar

¼ cup soy sauce or tamari

2 Tbsp honey

2 carrots, peeled and julienned

2 stalks celery, julienned

2 baby bok choy, halved and thinly sliced

1 lb/500 g skirt steak or boneless chicken breasts, thinly sliced across the grain (see Norene's Notes, below)

6 scallions, thinly sliced

toasted sesame seeds, for garnish

Method

1. Cook noodles according to package directions. Drain and rinse well. Set aside.

2. In a large soup pot, combine broth, rice vinegar, soy sauce, and honey. Bring to a boil; simmer, uncovered, for 5 minutes.

3. Add carrots, celery, bok choy, and steak. Reduce heat. Simmer, uncovered, for 5-7 minutes, until meat is cooked through. Stir occasionally.

4. Stir in cooked noodles and scallions. Adjust seasonings to taste. Garnish with sesame seeds.

Norene's Notes

- It's easier to cut beef into paper-thin slices if you partially freeze it first. The thinner the slice, the quicker it cooks.
- Short Cut: Use meat or chicken stir-fry as a substitute. Vegetarians can use the vegetable broth and substitute meat with diced firm tofu.

Green Soup Bowl

meat | pareve option | gluten-free | yields 6-8 servings

Ingredients

8 cups chicken or vegetable broth

2 stalks celery, sliced on the diagonal

2 cups green beans, trimmed and sliced on the diagonal

2 cups snow peas, trimmed and sliced on the diagonal

2 cups fresh or frozen broccoli florets

2 cups frozen shelled edamame beans

1-2 tsp kosher salt

freshly ground black pepper

chives or scallions, for garnish

Method

1. Bring broth to a boil in a large pot; reduce to simmer.

2. Add celery, green beans, snow peas, broccoli, edamame beans, salt, and pepper. Cook for 7 minutes, or until vegetables are tender-crisp. Do not overcook. Adjust seasonings to taste.

3. Garnish with chives. Serve immediately.

Norene's Notes

- Homemade Vegetable Broth: Cut into chunks 2 onions, 4 carrots, 4 stalks celery, 3 parsnips, 1 red bell pepper, 2-3 cloves garlic, ½ cup fresh dill. Add to a large pot with 2 tsp salt and ¼ tsp pepper. Add water to cover by 1 inch. Bring to a boil, partly covered; simmer 45 minutes. For clear broth, strain out vegetables. For thicker broth, purée vegetables.

The earthy richness of this soup gives it a rustic elegance. Its creamy texture, combined with morsels of meaty mushrooms, will have everyone asking for more!

Marvelous Mushroom Soup

pareve | passover | gluten-free | freezes well | yields 8 servings

Ingredients

2 Tbsp olive oil

2 large onions, diced

12 portobello mushroom caps (about 4 inches in diameter), sliced (see Norene's Notes, below)

4 cloves garlic, minced (about 2 tsp)

2 tsp minced fresh thyme leaves

2 tsp kosher salt

freshly ground black pepper

5-6 cups water or vegetable broth

additional thyme leaves, for garnish

Method

1. Heat oil in a large soup pot over medium-high heat. Add onions and sauté for 5 minutes or until golden.

2. Add mushrooms and stir-fry for 7-8 minutes or until golden.

3. Reduce heat to low and add garlic, thyme, salt, and pepper. Cook slowly until the onions have caramelized, 8-10 minutes, stirring occasionally.

4. Add water; bring to a boil. Reduce heat. Simmer, partially covered, for 20-25 minutes, stirring occasionally. Remove from heat; cool slightly.

5. Using an immersion blender, process soup until partially puréed. If soup is too thick, add a little water or broth. Adjust seasonings to taste. Garnish with thyme leaves.

Norene's Notes

- No portobellos? Substitute with button, cremini, or wild mushrooms. (Portobellos are actually a larger version of creminis.)
- Rinse mushrooms quickly before cooking, then wrap them in a towel to absorb moisture. Alternatively, clean mushrooms by wiping them with a damp cloth, or use a mushroom brush.

The unique pairing of parsnips and apples gives this soup the heartiness that warms you to your bones. The beautiful soup adds a nice touch to a wintery table setting, so I like to serve it around the time of the first snowfall.

Parsnip & Apple Soup

pareve | passover | gluten-free | freezes well | yields 8 servings

Ingredients

2 Tbsp olive oil

2 medium onions, diced

2 cloves garlic, minced (about 1 tsp)

2 lb/1 kg parsnips, peeled and cut into chunks (about 6 cups)

2 apples (e.g., McIntosh), peeled, cored, and cut into chunks

2 potatoes, peeled and cut into chunks

2 Tbsp brown sugar

2 tsp kosher salt

freshly ground black pepper

4-5 cups water or vegetable broth

1 tsp minced fresh thyme leaves

Method

1. Heat oil in a large soup pot over medium-high heat. Add onions and garlic; sauté for 5 minutes, or until softened.

2. Stir in parsnips, apples, potatoes, brown sugar, salt, pepper, and water. Bring to a boil.

3. Reduce heat. Simmer, partially covered, for 30-40 minutes, or until vegetables are tender. Stir occasionally. Remove from heat; cool slightly. Add thyme.

4. Using an immersion blender, process soup until smooth. If soup is too thick, add a little water or broth. Adjust seasonings to taste.

Norene's Notes

- Always peel parsnips. The bigger they are, the more bitter they are.
- Small, tender parsnips are delicious when grated and added raw to salads. A squeeze of lemon juice will prevent them from turning dark.
- Make our apple chip garnish: Preheat oven to 225°F. Slice 2 unpeeled apples paper thin; sprinkle with 2 tsp sugar, if desired. Bake for about 1½-2 hours, until crisp.

Perfect for a cool autumn evening, this bright soup has a sweet, warm flavor and a rich, creamy consistency.

Sweet Potato & Squash Soup

pareve | passover | gluten-free | freezes well | yields 8 servings

Ingredients

1 Tbsp olive oil

1 large onion, diced

1 butternut squash (about 3 lb/1.4 kg), peeled and cut into chunks (see Norene's Notes, below)

3 large sweet potatoes, peeled and cut into chunks

3 Tbsp honey

2 tsp kosher salt

freshly ground black pepper

6 cups water or vegetable broth

1 tsp minced fresh thyme leaves

additional thyme leaves, for garnish

Method

1. Heat oil in a large soup pot over medium heat. Add onion; sauté for 5 minutes, or until softened.

2. Stir in squash, sweet potatoes, honey, salt, pepper, and water. Bring to a boil.

3. Reduce heat. Simmer, partially covered, for 45 minutes or until vegetables are tender. Stir occasionally.

4. Add thyme. Remove soup from heat. Cool slightly.

5. Using an immersion blender, process soup until smooth. If soup is too thick, add a little water or broth. Adjust seasonings to taste. Garnish with thyme.

Norene's Notes

- To cut squash into chunks easily, try this easy trick. Slash squash in several places with a sharp knife. Microwave for 5 minutes on high (or bake at 350°F for 15-20 minutes). Cool slightly. Cut squash into two pieces at the neck. Cut the round bottom part in half. Using a large spoon, scoop out and discard seeds and stringy fiber. Peel squash with a vegetable peeler; cut into chunks.

Replacing noodles with spaghetti squash is such a brilliant idea! Hearty and filling, you'd never guess that this soup is vegetarian. What an easy way to guarantee you're getting those nutrients you need. It's a vitamin pill in a bowl!

Vegetable Soup
with spaghetti squash noodles
pareve | passover | gluten-free | yields 10 servings

Ingredients

1 medium spaghetti squash (about 3 lb/ 1.4 kg)

2 Tbsp olive oil

2 medium onions, diced

2 cups mushrooms, sliced

4 cloves garlic, minced (about 2 tsp)

2 sweet potatoes, peeled and cut into chunks

3 carrots, peeled and sliced

3 stalks celery, sliced

2 medium zucchini, cut into half-moons (do not peel)

1 Tbsp kosher salt

freshly ground black pepper

6 cups water or vegetable broth

2 Tbsp chopped fresh basil

Method

1. Preheat oven to 375°F. Line a baking sheet with parchment paper.

2. **Noodles:** For short strands, cut squash in half lengthwise; for long strands, cut it into 1-inch rings. Discard seeds and pulp. Place squash, cut side down, on prepared baking sheet. Bake, uncovered, for 35-45 minutes, or until tender.

3. **Soup:** Meanwhile, heat oil in a large soup pot over medium heat. Add onions, mushrooms, and garlic; sauté for 6-8 minutes, or until golden.

4. Add sweet potatoes, carrots, celery, and zucchini; stir in salt and pepper. Add water. Bring to a boil; reduce heat. Simmer, partially covered, for 30-35 minutes, or until vegetables are tender.

5. Add chopped basil. Simmer until heated through; adjust seasonings. Ladle soup into bowls. Use a fork to separate squash strands; add a portion to each to bowl.

Norene's Notes

• A 3 lb/1.4 kg spaghetti squash yields about 4 cups cooked.

• To cut squash in half easily, microwave it for 5 minutes on high. (No need to cut slashes in it because the cooking time is so short.)

This nutritious and delicious soup comes together quickly. I often make it in advance, but it thickens quite a bit, so when reheating it, I slowly add water until I get the right creamy consistency.

Cauliflower Lentil Soup

pareve | gluten-free | freezes well | yields 8 servings

Ingredients

1-2 Tbsp olive oil

2 onions, chopped

3 cloves garlic, minced (about 1½ tsp)

2 carrots, peeled and chopped

2 stalks celery, chopped

½ red bell pepper, chopped

1 cup dry red lentils, rinsed and drained

1 tsp cumin

1 tsp turmeric

1 bay leaf

6 cups water or vegetable broth

4 cups cauliflower florets

2 tsp kosher salt

¼ **tsp** black pepper

diced red bell pepper, for garnish

Method

1. Heat oil in a large soup pot over medium heat. Add onions and garlic; sauté for 5 minutes, or until softened.

2. Stir in carrots, celery, bell pepper, lentils, cumin, turmeric, and bay leaf. Add water; bring to a boil.

3. Reduce heat and simmer, partially covered, for 30-35 minutes, or until lentils are nearly tender, stirring occasionally.

4. Add cauliflower, salt, and pepper. Simmer for an additional 15 minutes.

5. Remove from heat and cool slightly. Remove bay leaf.

6. Using an immersion blender, process soup until smooth. If soup is too thick, add a little water or broth. Adjust seasonings to taste. Garnish with diced red pepper.

Norene's Notes

- When cooking legumes such as lentils or beans, don't add the salt until the last few minutes of cooking or the legumes won't become soft.
- A food processor will chop the vegetables in moments. Work in batches, if necessary. Use quick on/off pulses to prevent them from becoming over-processed.

Salads

For nutritional information on this section, see pages 321–322

When I plan a vegetarian menu, this Tex-Mex inspired salad tops my list. It's colorful, light, and delicious, and packed with the health benefits of edamame and black beans. See Norene's Notes, below, on using fresh corn in season.

Edamame, Corn & Black Bean Salad

pareve | gluten-free | yields 8 servings

Ingredients

1 pkg (12 oz/340 g) frozen shelled edamame beans

2 cans (12 oz/340 ml each) corn niblets, drained and rinsed

1 can (19 oz/540 ml) black beans, drained and rinsed

2 Tbsp chopped fresh mint or cilantro

Dressing

⅓ cup extra virgin olive oil

2 tsp lime zest

½ cup lime juice (preferably fresh)

1 tsp kosher salt, or to taste

freshly ground black pepper

Method

1. Bring a medium saucepan of salted water to a boil. Add edamame beans and boil for 3-5 minutes, until tender-crisp. Drain well. Place in a bowl of ice-cold water for a few minutes to help retain their bright green color. Drain well and pat dry.

2. In a large bowl, combine edamame beans with corn and black beans. Add mint.

3. Add dressing ingredients; toss well. Cover; refrigerate until serving time.

Norene's Notes

- Using a lime dressing is like tossing your salad in vitamin C. The acid in limes is antibacterial and promotes good digestive health, plus it's great for your skin and hair!
- One lime yields 1 teaspoon zest and 2 tablespoons juice. Always zest the lime first; then squeeze out the juice. Lime zest freezes well.
- Variation: Add 1 avocado, halved, pitted, and diced, shortly before serving.
- When fresh corn is in season, use 3-4 ears, cooked in lightly salted boiling water for 8-10 minutes. Use a sharp knife to shave off kernels.

This magnificent magenta salad is packed with vitamins, minerals, and almost everything else you need. Each ingredient has its place: something crunchy, something smooth, something tangy, something sweet, something leafy. Perfect!

Roasted Beet Salad
with lemon-basil dressing

pareve | dairy option | passover | gluten-free | yields 8 servings

Ingredients

2 bunches red or rainbow beets, scrubbed and trimmed (about 8 medium)

½ medium red onion, quartered and thinly sliced

¼ cup extra virgin olive oil

¼ cup lemon juice (preferably fresh)

2 Tbsp honey

¼ cup chopped fresh basil

½ tsp kosher salt, or to taste

freshly ground black pepper

6 cups micro greens or mixed greens

⅓ cup shelled pistachios, coarsely chopped

¾ cup crumbled goat cheese (optional)

Method

1. Preheat oven to 350°F.

2. Coat a large piece of heavy-duty foil with nonstick cooking spray. Center beets on foil; wrap tightly, pinching edges together.

3. Bake for 1-1½ hours, or until tender (see Norene's Notes, below). Carefully open packet and let beets stand until cool enough to handle.

4. Using paper towels, rub off and discard skins. Slice beets into wedges. Place into a large bowl; add onion.

5. Add oil, lemon juice, honey, basil, salt, and pepper to the bowl; toss to combine. Cover and refrigerate. (Can be done up to a day in advance.)

6. Arrange a layer of greens on a large serving platter. Top with dressed beets. Scatter pistachios and goat cheese, if using, over salad.

Norene's Notes

• For even cooking, choose fresh beets that are approximately the same size. Small to medium-size beets are more tender, while larger beets tend to be tough. Beets are fully cooked when a metal skewer glides through them easily.

This crunchy salad wins major points: It's super-delicious, with all the right flavors and textures. Massaging kale transforms the leathery leaves into a sweet, delicate salad.

Red Cabbage & Kale Salad

pareve | gluten-free | yields 8 servings

Ingredients

1 medium bunch kale (about 1 lb/500 g)

1 pkg (16 oz/500 g) sliced red cabbage

1 can (14 oz/400 g) sliced hearts of palm, drained and rinsed

½ cup toasted sunflower or pumpkin seeds (see Norene's Notes, below)

Dressing

¼ cup extra virgin olive oil

¼ cup rice vinegar

3 Tbsp soy sauce or tamari

2 Tbsp honey or pure maple syrup

½ tsp kosher salt, or to taste

freshly ground black pepper

Method

1. Wash and dry kale. Remove and discard tough stalks and center veins. Massage kale with your fingertips for about 5 minutes, until leaves have wilted. Chop into bite-sized pieces.

2. Combine kale with cabbage and hearts of palm in a large bowl. Cover and chill.

3. **Dressing:** Combine dressing ingredients in a glass jar; seal tightly and shake well. Refrigerate.

4. Toss salad with dressing shortly before serving. Top with sunflower or pumpkin seeds.

Norene's Notes

- To toast sunflower or pumpkin seeds, spread in a 9-inch pie plate and bake in a preheated 350°F oven for 5-7 minutes, until fragrant.
- If you have both sunflower and pumpkin seeds on hand, use a combination.

This low-cal salad is my go-to vegetable choice for a lighter addition to a heavier meal. The raw vegetables and fresh herbs put a garden-fresh spin on traditional cucumber salad by brightening the flavor and adding extra crunch.

Crunchy Celery & Cucumber Salad

pareve | passover | gluten-free | yields 8-10 servings

Ingredients

6 stalks celery, thinly sliced

12 baby cucumbers, thinly sliced (do not peel)

8 red radishes, thinly sliced (do not peel)

½ cup thinly sliced red onion

4 scallions, thinly sliced

½ cup chopped fresh parsley

¼ cup chopped fresh dill

Dressing

⅓ cup extra virgin olive oil

⅓ cup red wine vinegar

1 Tbsp honey

3 cloves garlic, minced (about 1½ tsp)

1½ tsp kosher salt, or to taste

freshly ground black pepper

Method

1. In a large serving bowl, combine celery, cucumbers, radishes, red onion, scallions, parsley, and dill.

2. **Dressing:** Combine dressing ingredients in a glass jar; seal tightly and shake well.

3. Add dressing to salad; mix well. Cover; refrigerate until serving time.

Norene's Notes

- How to store fresh herbs: Wrap fresh herbs (e.g., parsley, dill) in damp paper towels. Place in a resealable plastic bag; refrigerate. They will keep 4-5 days.

- No fresh herbs? Chop equal parts of fresh parsley with the dried herb. The parsley will take on the flavor of the dried herb, and the dried herb will taste fresher. You can also substitute approximately 1 teaspoon dried herbs for each tablespoon of fresh herbs.

- Mince a batch of fresh herbs in a food processor or mini prep. Drop in blobs onto parchment paper and freeze; then transfer to resealable freezer bags. They're ready when you are! P.S. Be sure to mark the package so you know what's inside.

This fabulous salad is a staple in my house —
it looks and tastes phenomenal and is always a
crowd pleaser. For a grilled, smoky flavor, place
the boiled corn on the barbecue grill for a few
minutes, then shave off the kernels in long strips.

Shaved Corn & Asparagus Salad

pareve | gluten-free | yields 8 servings

Ingredients

8 ears corn, husked and cleaned

1 bunch asparagus (snap off and discard tough ends)

1 cup cherry tomatoes, halved

¼ cup chopped fresh basil

Dressing

⅓ cup extra virgin olive oil

⅓ cup lemon juice (preferably fresh)

4 cloves garlic, minced (about 2 tsp)

1 tsp kosher salt, or to taste

freshly ground black pepper

Method

1. Bring a large pot of lightly salted water to a boil. Add corn and cook for 5 minutes. Add asparagus; continue cooking for additional 3-5 minutes, until tender-crisp. Drain corn and asparagus; place in ice-cold water for 5 minutes. Drain and pat dry.

2. Shave off corn kernels with a sharp knife, leaving them attached to each other, if possible. Place into a large serving bowl.

3. Cut asparagus into 1-inch pieces and add to corn along with tomatoes and basil.

4. **Dressing:** Combine dressing ingredients in a glass jar; seal tightly and shake well.

5. Add dressing to salad. Toss gently to combine. Cover, refrigerate until shortly before serving time. Adjust seasonings to taste.

Norene's Notes

- When corn on the cob is not an option, use frozen corn kernels. Cook 5-6 cups frozen corn in boiling water for 3-4 minutes. Drain well and pat dry. Canned corn niblets are also an excellent option.

- If using fresh corn, stand it upright on its base so the corn is stable. Shave off the kernels with a sharp knife — or even a shoehorn!

Although it calls for only a few ingredients, this colorful salad is packed with crunch and flavor. The subtle licorice flavor of fennel, the spice of radish, plus the hint of sweet tartness from the cranberries pair well with almost any main course.

Fennel & Radish Salad

pareve | passover | gluten-free | yields 8 servings

Ingredients

2 medium fennel bulbs, halved, cored, and thinly sliced (see Norene's Notes, below)

6 red radishes, thinly sliced

¼ cup thinly sliced red onion

½ cup dried cranberries

Dressing

⅓ cup extra virgin olive oil

¼ cup lemon juice (preferably fresh)

1 Tbsp honey

1 tsp kosher salt, or to taste

freshly ground black pepper

Method

1. In a large serving bowl, combine fennel with radishes and red onion.

2. **Dressing:** Combine dressing ingredients in a glass jar; seal tightly and shake well.

3. Add dressing to bowl; toss well to combine. Cover and refrigerate.

4. Toss in dried cranberries shortly before serving.

Norene's Notes

• How to prepare fennel: Remove stems and fronds from fennel. Trim away any tough or blemished outer layers from the bulb. Trim off and discard the base. Cut bulb in half; remove and discard core. The feathery fronds can be minced and added to the salad.

• For extra crunch, add 1 large Gala or Red Delicious apple, cored and thinly sliced. Sprinkle with a few drops of lemon juice to prevent discoloration.

This recipe is courtesy of my jet-setting friend, Chantal Ulmer. After a trip to Turks and Caicos, she said this salad was the best thing she'd eaten. Exotic, light, refreshing — this mix of fruits and veggies is unbelievably delicious.

Exotic Island Salad

pareve | gluten-free | yields 6-8 servings

Ingredients

3 ears corn, husked and cleaned

6 baby cucumbers, halved lengthwise and cut into long, thin strips (do not peel)

1 firm Asian pear, halved, cored, and thinly sliced (do not peel)

1 large jicama, peeled, halved, and cut into long, thin strips

Dressing

⅓ cup extra virgin olive oil

½ cup lime juice, (preferably fresh, from about 4 limes)

2 Tbsp chopped fresh mint or basil

1 tsp kosher salt, or to taste

freshly ground black pepper

Method

1. Bring a large pot of lightly salted water to a boil. Add corn and cook for 6-8 minutes. Drain well; cool slightly and pat dry.

2. Shave off corn kernels with a sharp knife, leaving them attached to each other if possible. Place into a serving bowl. Add cucumbers, Asian pear, and jicama.

3. Dressing: Combine dressing ingredients in a glass jar; seal tightly and shake well.

4. Add dressing to salad and mix well. Cover; refrigerate until serving time.

Norene's Notes

• Asian pears have a similar texture to apples as they have a crisp, crunchy texture.

• If Asian pears are not available, use crisp, firm apples or pears. Mango would also be delicious in this salad.

One of the most important cooking lessons that I learned from my Mom, Resa Litwack, was how to make simple food taste delicious. Healthy and flavorful, this scrumptious salad takes minutes to prepare and pairs well with almost everything.

Lentil Cranberry Salad

pareve | gluten-free | yields 6 servings

Ingredients

2 cans (19 oz/540 ml each) lentils, drained and rinsed

⅓ cup red onion, diced

⅓ cup extra virgin olive oil

juice of **2** lemons (about 1/3 cup)

2 cloves garlic, minced (about 1 tsp)

1 tsp kosher salt, or to taste

freshly ground black pepper

½ cup dried cranberries

Method

1. Combine lentils and onion in a medium bowl.

2. Add oil, lemon juice, garlic, salt, and pepper; toss well. Cover and refrigerate.

3. Stir in dried cranberries just before serving. Adjust seasonings to taste.

Norene's Notes

- Canned lentils are convenient and nutritious, but are more expensive than dried and are generally higher in sodium. To cook your own, combine 2 cups brown lentils with 6 cups cold unsalted water in a large saucepan. Bring to a boil, cover, and simmer until tender, 30-35 minutes. Drain well. Makes 4 cups.
- Variation: Substitute red kidney beans for lentils. So pretty.

My kids love mangoes so much that I buy 10 each week. This salad is perfect for a barbecue and pairs really well with grilled chicken or beef. To get that juicy, sweet flavor, make sure to use ripe mangoes.

Fresh Mango Salad

pareve | passover | gluten-free | yields 6-8 servings

Ingredients

5 ripe mangoes, peeled and cut into long narrow slices (see Norene's Notes, below)

½ cup thinly sliced red onion

½ cup chopped fresh parsley

2 Tbsp chopped fresh basil

Dressing

¼ cup extra virgin olive oil

¼ cup lemon juice (preferably fresh)

1 Tbsp brown sugar

½ tsp kosher salt, or to taste

freshly ground black pepper

Method

1. In a large bowl, combine mangoes with red onion, parsley, and basil.

2. **Dressing:** Combine dressing ingredients in a glass jar; seal tightly and shake well.

3. Add dressing and mix well. Cover and refrigerate until ready to serve.

Norene's Notes

- How to slice a mango: Using a sharp knife, cut down one side of the mango, feeling for the pit with your knife. Repeat on the other side, making two large pieces. Slice mango flesh into long, narrow slices — but don't cut right through to the skin. Cut mango slices away from the skin.

- How to dice a mango: Score the mango flesh into dice, but don't cut right through to the skin. Bend each mango piece backward and cut the flesh away from the skin.

- For a sweeter flavor, use ¼ cup mango juice instead of lemon juice.

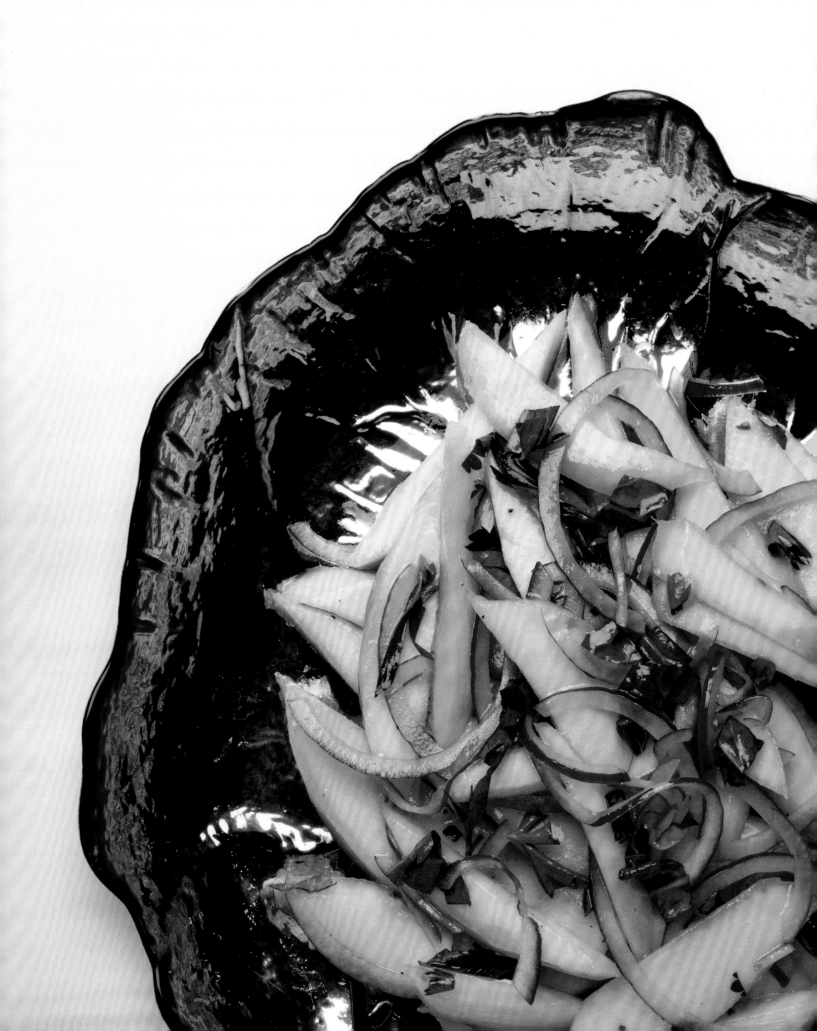

This all-in-one salad is high in protein and rich in minerals, so it can hold its own as a light meal. It's also great to serve as a side dish for gluten-free guests, and perfect for packing into lunches, too.

Green Salad
with mushrooms & quinoa
pareve | passover | gluten-free | yields 6-8 servings

Ingredients

1⅓ cups lightly salted water

⅔ cup quinoa

1-2 Tbsp olive oil

2 cups assorted mushrooms, thinly sliced

2 Tbsp balsamic vinegar

6 cups mixed salad greens

1 cup cherry tomatoes, halved

1 ripe Hass avocado (see Norene's Notes, below)

Dressing

¼ cup extra virgin olive oil

¼ cup balsamic vinegar

2 cloves garlic, minced (about 1 tsp)

1 tsp minced fresh thyme leaves

½ tsp kosher salt, or to taste

freshly ground black pepper

Method

1. Bring water to a boil in a medium saucepan. Add quinoa; reduce heat. Simmer, covered, for 15 minutes or until tender. Let stand, covered, for 10 minutes. Fluff with a fork. Transfer to a large serving bowl and let cool.

2. In a large nonstick skillet, heat oil over medium-high heat. Sauté mushrooms for 6-8 minutes or until golden. Stir in balsamic vinegar and cook 1-2 minutes longer. Let cool. Drain excess liquid, if necessary.

3. Add mushrooms, mixed greens, and cherry tomatoes to quinoa. Cover and chill.

4. Dressing: Combine dressing ingredients in a glass jar; seal tightly and shake well. Refrigerate.

5. Dice avocado shortly before serving. Toss salad with dressing; add avocado just before serving.

Norene's Notes

- Nice dice: Cut avocado in half lengthwise and gently twist the two halves back and forth until you can separate them. Remove pit (carefully stick the knife into pit and twist the knife back and forth until the pit loosens). Dice avocado flesh right in its shell without cutting through to the skin. Scoop out avocado flesh with a spoon.

This gorgeous salad is refreshing, clean, and simple. As an almost-all-green salad with very few ingredients, the unique cut on the sweet snap peas exposing the tiny green treasures hidden within makes it so elegant to present.

Snap Pea Salad
with basil-mint dressing

pareve | gluten-free | yields 8 servings

Ingredients

2 cups sugar snap peas, trimmed, strings removed

8 cups mixed salad greens

½ cup thinly sliced red onion

6 radishes, thinly sliced

Dressing

⅓ cup extra virgin olive oil

⅓ cup lemon juice (preferably fresh)

1 Tbsp honey

1 clove garlic, minced (about ½ tsp)

2 Tbsp chopped fresh mint

2 Tbsp chopped fresh basil

½ tsp kosher salt, or to taste

freshly ground black pepper

Method

1. Cut snap pea pods in half lengthwise so peas are exposed. There will be some peas on each side of the pod.

2. In a large bowl, combine pea pods with salad greens, red onion, and radishes. Cover and chill.

3. Dressing: Combine dressing ingredients in a glass jar; seal tightly and shake well. Refrigerate.

4. Gently toss salad with dressing just before serving.

Norene's Notes

• Sugar snap peas are also known as mangetout (French for "eat all"). They are usually used in stir-fries, but this creative presentation looks magnificent in salads.

• Snow peas have a flatter shape, while sugar snap peas are rounded.

I serve this summer salad at barbecues or at dinner parties. The tangy dressing balances the bold flavors of spinach and avocado, and the candied nuts add a lasting sweetness. It's the perfect dish for lazy summer days.

Candied Nut Spinach Salad

pareve | gluten-free | yield 8 servings

Ingredients

3 ears corn, husked and cleaned

8 cups baby spinach

1 pint cherry tomatoes, halved

1 ripe Hass avocado

1 cup chopped candied pecans or almonds (p. 280)

Dressing

⅓ cup extra virgin olive oil

¼ cup balsamic vinegar

2 Tbsp lemon juice (preferably fresh)

2 cloves garlic, minced (about 1 tsp)

½ tsp kosher salt, or to taste

freshly ground black pepper

Method

1. Bring a large pot of lightly salted water to a boil. Add corn and boil for 8-10 minutes, until tender. Drain well. Place corn into a bowl of ice-cold water for 5 minutes. Drain well and pat dry.

2. Shave off corn kernels with a sharp knife, leaving them attached to each other, if possible; place them into a large serving bowl. Top with spinach and tomatoes. Cover and chill.

3. **Dressing:** Combine dressing ingredients in a glass jar, seal tightly, and shake well. Refrigerate.

4. Peel, pit, and dice avocado shortly before serving. Toss salad with avocado, nuts, and dressing just before serving.

Norene's Notes

- Keep unripe avocados on the counter: they will ripen within a few days. To speed ripening, place avocado into a paper bag with a banana. When ripe, the avocado will give slightly when you press it gently.

- If you don't plan on eating a ripe avocado right away, put it into the refrigerator to stop the ripening process.

In this simple salad, dill adds a pleasantly fresh flavor. I use ripe heirloom tomatoes when they are available, but cherry or grape tomatoes are easier to find. This salad multiplies easily.

Tomato Dill Salad

pareve | passover option | dairy option | gluten-free | yields 6-8 servings

Ingredients

3 pints cherry or grape tomatoes, halved

6 scallions, thinly sliced

⅓ cup chopped fresh dill

Dressing

⅓ cup extra virgin olive oil

1 tsp fresh lemon zest

⅓ cup lemon juice (preferably fresh)

2 tsp Dijon mustard (omit for Passover)

½ tsp kosher salt, or to taste

freshly ground black pepper

Method

1. In a large serving bowl, combine tomatoes, scallions, and dill.

2. **Dressing:** Combine dressing ingredients in a glass jar; seal tightly and shake well.

3. Add dressing to salad; mix well. Serve chilled.

Norene's Notes

- Variation: Add 4 baby cucumbers, diced.
- Dairy Variation: Add 1 cup baby bocconcini balls, halved. An easy alternative is mozzarella cheese sticks, cut into half-inch slices.
- When a recipe calls for citrus zest and juice, first grate the fruit, then squeeze out the juice. You can freeze any extra zest and juice for future use.

Sweet, tangy, and perfect for a backyard barbecue, this simple slaw will transport you to a mini Hawaiian getaway. The cabbage and almonds offer a satisfying crunch, while the pineapple brings a tropical punch.

Hawaiian Coleslaw

pareve | passover option | gluten-free | yields 8 servings

Ingredients

1 pkg (16 oz/500 g) sliced red cabbage

1 pkg (16 oz/500 g) sliced green cabbage

1 red bell pepper, diced

½ red onion, diced

2 scallions, thinly sliced

2 Tbsp chopped fresh basil (or 1 tsp dried)

2 cups pineapple chunks (fresh or canned)

¾ cup candied whole or slivered almonds (optional) (p. 280)

Dressing

⅓ cup olive oil

⅓ cup vinegar (see Norene's Notes, below)

2 Tbsp honey

2 tsp kosher salt, or to taste

¼ tsp black pepper

Method

1. In a large bowl, combine cabbages, red pepper, onion, scallions, and basil.

2. **Dressing:** In a medium saucepan, combine dressing ingredients; bring to a boil.

3. Pour hot dressing over cabbage mixture; toss well. Cover and refrigerate until serving time.

4. Toss coleslaw with pineapple and candied almonds, if using, shortly before serving.

Norene's Notes

- Pouring hot dressing over the cabbage mixture eliminates the sulfur smell that develops in leftover coleslaw.
- Red cabbage looks beautiful in this coleslaw. When you pour the hot dressing over red cabbage, it will turn a beautiful magenta color.
- Passover Option: Use Passover vinegar or lemon juice in the dressing.

Roasted sweet potatoes bring hearty texture to this fresh kale salad while keeping things light and simple. Tossed with a salty-sweet dressing and topped with a touch of tart cranberry flavor, this salad makes a colorful side dish.

Kale Salad
with roasted sweet potatoes
pareve | gluten-free | yields 8 servings

Ingredients

2 sweet potatoes, peeled and diced

1 Tbsp olive oil

kosher salt

freshly ground black pepper

1 bunch kale (about 1 lb/500 g)

1 cup dried cranberries

Dressing

¼ cup extra virgin olive oil

¼ cup rice vinegar

2 Tbsp soy sauce or tamari

2 Tbsp pure maple syrup

½ tsp kosher salt, or to taste

freshly ground black pepper

Method

1. Preheat oven to 400°F. Line a baking sheet with parchment paper.

2. Spread sweet potatoes on prepared baking sheet. Drizzle with oil and sprinkle with salt and pepper.

3. Roast, uncovered, for 25-30 minutes or until tender. Let cool.

4. Wash and dry kale. Remove and discard tough stalks and center veins. Massage kale with your fingertips for about 5 minutes, until leaves are wilted. Chop into bite-sized pieces and place into a large serving bowl. Cover and chill.

5. **Dressing:** Combine dressing ingredients in a glass jar; seal tightly and shake well. Refrigerate.

6. Add sweet potatoes and cranberries to kale; toss with dressing just before serving.

Norene's Notes

- The darker the flesh, the sweeter and moister the sweet potatoes will be. They are delicious baked, boiled, steamed, grilled, or roasted.
- Because of their lower glycemic index, sweet potatoes are a carb-friendly choice for people with diabetes or insulin resistance.

Fish

For nutritional information on this section, see page 322

These recipes are made with pantry essentials and take almost no time to prepare. Each pairs perfectly with almost any side dish and can easily be multiplied, so any version makes a great dish to whip together for a crowd. As a bonus, each freezes well!

Sticky Sesame Salmon

pareve | gluten-free | yields 6-8 servings

Ingredients

½ **cup** honey

3 Tbsp soy sauce or tamari

4 cloves garlic, minced (about 2 tsp)

juice of ½ lemon (about 2 Tbsp)

¼ **cup** sesame seeds, plus extra for garnish

6-8 salmon fillets (about 6 oz/180 g each)

Method

1. In a small bowl, stir together honey, soy sauce, garlic, lemon juice, and sesame seeds.

2. Preheat oven to 425°F. Line a rimmed baking sheet with foil; coat with nonstick cooking spray.

3. Arrange salmon in a single layer on prepared baking sheet. Drizzle sauce over fish. Let stand for 20 minutes, if time allows.

4. Bake, uncovered, for 12-15 minutes, basting occasionally, until salmon is glazed and golden.

5. Garnish with sesame seeds. Serve hot or at room temperature.

Norene's Notes

• Salmon fillets often have pin bones that should be removed before cooking. To remove them easily, drape the salmon, flesh-side up, over an inverted curved bowl. The bones will protrude and will be easy to remove with a pair of tweezers.

Balsamic Honey-Glazed Salmon

pareve | gluten-free | yields 4-6 servings

Ingredients

⅓ **cup** balsamic vinegar

3 Tbsp honey

1 Tbsp Dijon mustard

4 cloves garlic, minced (about 2 tsp)

4-6 salmon fillets (about 6 oz/180 g each)

2 scallions, sliced (or Scallion Brushes; see Norene's Notes, below), for garnish

Method

1. In a small bowl, stir together balsamic vinegar, honey, mustard, and garlic.

2. Preheat oven to 425°F. Line a rimmed baking sheet with foil; coat with nonstick cooking spray.

3. Arrange salmon in a single layer on prepared baking sheet. Pour sauce over fish. Let stand for 20 minutes, if time allows.

4. Bake, uncovered, for 12-15 minutes, basting occasionally, until salmon is glazed and golden. Serve hot or at room temperature. Garnish with scallions or Scallion Brushes.

Norene's Notes

• Scallion Brushes: Cut off most of the green part of scallions; trim the root ends, leaving bulbs intact. Scallions should then be about 4 inches long. Cut 1-inch slits at each end. Place scallions into ice-cold water for 30 minutes; ends will fan out and curl.

Maple-Glazed Salmon

pareve | gluten-free | yields 4-6 servings

Ingredients

⅓ cup pure maple syrup

3 Tbsp soy sauce or tamari

2 cloves garlic, minced (about 1 tsp)

juice of **½** lemon (about 2 Tbsp)

4-6 salmon fillets (about 6 oz/180 g each)

Method

1. In a small bowl, stir together maple syrup, soy sauce, garlic, and lemon juice.

2. Preheat oven to 425°F. Line a rimmed baking sheet with foil; coat with nonstick cooking spray.

3. Arrange salmon in a single layer on prepared baking sheet. Pour sauce over fish. Let stand for 20 minutes, if time allows.

4. Bake, uncovered, for 12-15 minutes, basting occasionally, until salmon is glazed and golden. Serve hot or at room temperature.

Norene's Notes

- Store unopened maple syrup in a cool, dry place. Once opened, store tightly closed in the refrigerator. For long-term storage, you can freeze maple syrup. It won't solidify, but it will become very thick.

Grilling on a cedar plank is a simple way to cook and serve salmon, infusing it with a subtle smokiness. Strawberries make a perfect counterpoint to the salsa's chili pepper. The plank keeps the fish warm while serving.

Cedar-Planked Salmon
with strawberry-chili salsa

pareve | passover | gluten-free | freezes well; do not freeze salsa | yields 4-6 servings

Ingredients

Special equipment

1 or 2 untreated cedar planks (about 12 x 7-inches)

Salsa

2 cups diced strawberries

⅓ cup diced red onion

2 Tbsp chopped fresh mint or basil

1 Tbsp extra virgin olive oil

juice of **1** lime (about 2 Tbsp)

1 serrano or jalapeño chili pepper, finely diced (remove seeds first for less heat)

1 tsp kosher salt

¼ tsp black pepper

Fish

4-6 salmon fillets (about 6 oz/180 g each)

1-2 Tbsp olive oil

kosher salt

freshly ground black pepper

Method

1. Soak 1 or 2 cedar planks in cold water for at least 1 hour. Top planks with two or three unopened cans to keep them submerged while soaking.

2. **Salsa:** In a medium bowl, stir together strawberries, onion, mint, oil, lime juice, chili pepper, salt, and pepper. Cover and refrigerate.

3. **Fish:** Preheat grill to medium-high. Remove plank(s) from water and place on hot grate over indirect heat for 6-8 minutes, until hot. Using tongs, carefully turn plank(s) over and place salmon fillets on top. Brush fillets with oil; season with salt and pepper.

4. Cover grill and cook for 12-15 minutes or until salmon flakes when lightly pressed with a fork. It's not necessary to turn the salmon.

5. Remove from grill and spoon salsa over the salmon. Serve salmon directly from the plank(s).

Norene's Notes

- Oven Method: Place soaked planks onto a baking sheet. Top with salmon; brush fish with oil and season with salt and pepper. Bake in a preheated 425°F oven for 12-15 minutes. As the water evaporates from the plank(s), steam will be released, keeping the fish moist and aromatic.

This simple salmon dish is often on my menu when I have guests. The hint of mint is my unique signature, adding something unexpected to this classic dish. Squeeze a little lemon juice over the salmon before serving.

Herbed Salmon

pareve | passover | gluten-free | freezes well | yields 6-8 servings

Ingredients

1 skinless, boneless fillet of salmon (about 2 lb/1 kg)

kosher salt

freshly ground black pepper

1½ cups fresh parsley

1 cup fresh mint or basil

1½ cups fresh dill

6 scallions, trimmed

4 cloves garlic (about 2 tsp)

2 Tbsp olive oil

juice of **2** lemons (about 6-8 Tbsp)

1-2 Tbsp honey

Method

1. Preheat oven to 425°F. Line a rimmed baking sheet with aluminum foil; coat with nonstick cooking spray.

2. Place salmon onto prepared baking sheet. Sprinkle generously with salt and pepper.

3. Using a food processor or mini prep, process parsley, mint, dill, scallions, and garlic until coarsely chopped. Add oil, lemon juice, and honey; pulse briefly to combine.

4. Remove 3-4 Tbsp of herb mixture and set aside. Spread remaining herb mixture evenly over salmon. Let stand 20-30 minutes if time allows.

5. Bake, uncovered, for 15-18 minutes, or until salmon flakes when lightly pressed with a fork.

6. Transfer salmon fillet to an oblong serving platter or cut it into individual portions. Spoon on reserved herb mixture. Serve hot or at room temperature.

Norene's Notes

• Pantastic: An easy way to transfer a salmon fillet to a serving platter is to use a rimless baking sheet as a giant spatula!

My fish stick version is just as kid-friendly as the boxed version, minus the preservatives and additives. These have an irresistible cornflake crunch and a lemony dill flavor that adds a homemade freshness.

Halibut Fish Sticks

pareve | passover option | gluten-free option | freezes well | yields 4-6 servings

Ingredients

2 eggs

1 Tbsp oil

4 cups cornflakes (regular or gluten-free), lightly crushed

4-6 halibut fillets (about 6 oz/180 g each)

kosher salt

freshly ground black pepper

2 Tbsp minced fresh dill

lemon juice, for sprinkling

Method

1. Preheat oven to 450°F. Line a rimmed baking sheet with aluminum foil. Coat with nonstick cooking spray.

2. Lightly beat eggs with oil in a pie plate.

3. Place crushed cornflakes into a medium bowl.

4. Cut fish into strips about 3 inches long by ½-inch thick.

5. Season fish with salt, pepper, and dill. Dunk into egg, then coat on all sides with cornflakes; pressing gently will help them stick. Arrange fish in a single layer on prepared pan.

6. Bake, uncovered, for 10-12 minutes or until golden.

7. Sprinkle with lemon juice and serve.

Norene's Notes

- Adding oil to the eggs makes the fish sticks crispy without frying.
- Variation: Instead of cornflakes, use coarsely crushed pretzels (regular or gluten-free).
- Passover Option: Instead of cornflakes, use Passover soup mandlen (soup croutons), which are also available gluten-free. Matzo meal (regular or gluten-free) also works well.

Fresh, clean colors and perfectly balanced flavors make this a company-worthy starter salad. The tartness of the grapefruit, smoothed by the drizzle of honey in the dressing, adds a bright citrus aroma.

Halibut, Grapefruit & Spinach Salad

pareve | passover | gluten-free | yields 4 main dish or 8 appetizer servings

Ingredients

4 halibut, tilapia, or sole fillets (about 8 oz/250 g each)

1-2 Tbsp olive oil

kosher salt

freshly ground black pepper

Salad

6 cups baby spinach or arugula leaves

2 pink grapefruits, supremed (see Norene's Notes, below)

Dressing

¼ cup grapefruit juice (preferably fresh)

¼ cup extra virgin olive oil

1 Tbsp honey

kosher salt

freshly ground black pepper

Method

1. Preheat oven to 425°F. Line a rimmed baking sheet with parchment paper.

2. Place fish onto prepared baking sheet. Drizzle with olive oil; sprinkle generously with salt and pepper. Bake, uncovered, for 10-12 minutes, or until fish flakes with a fork. Let cool.

3. **Salad:** In a large bowl, combine spinach with grapefruit segments.

4. **Dressing:** Combine dressing ingredients in a glass jar; seal tightly and shake well.

5. Drizzle dressing over salad; toss to combine. Add halibut and mix gently, breaking fish into chunks.

Norene's Notes

• To supreme grapefruit: Cut a slice from the top and bottom of each grapefruit so it will be easier to peel. Slice off the peel and pith by following the curve of the fruit. Cut grapefruit into segments, removing flesh and discarding membrane and seeds. Do this over a bowl to catch the juice.

• Variation: Halibut, Mango & Spinach Salad: Instead of grapefruit, substitute 2 mangoes, peeled, pitted, and cut into thin strips. Use mango juice instead of grapefruit juice. Add 2 sliced baby cucumbers, and 1 diced avocado. Wow!

The delicate, flaky texture of sea bass is the perfect vessel for a sauce as silky, savory, and heavenly as this one. This dish landed a spot on my top ten list — it is absolutely amazing!

Sea Bass
with lemon butter sauce

dairy | passover | gluten-free | freezes well | yields 6 servings

Ingredients

6 sea bass (or black cod) fillets (6 oz/180 g each)

kosher salt

freshly ground black pepper

1 Tbsp olive oil

½ cup butter

6 large shallots, diced

1 Tbsp lemon zest

juice of **1** lemon (about 3-4 Tbsp)

Method

1. Preheat oven to 425°F. Line a rimmed baking sheet with parchment paper.

2. Place fillets onto prepared baking sheet. Season generously with salt and pepper; drizzle with olive oil.

3. Bake, uncovered, for 10-12 minutes, or until fish flakes when lightly pressed with a fork.

4. Meanwhile, melt butter over low heat in a medium skillet. Add shallots and lemon zest; sauté for 3-5 minutes, until softened. Squeeze in lemon juice.

5. Transfer fish to a serving platter or individual plates; pour sauce over fish.

Norene's Notes

- Shallots are small and round with a thin, papery skin. Most shallots actually contain two bulbs, so pull them apart to separate them. Peel away the papery skin with your fingertips.
- If you don't have shallots, substitute diced red onion.

Quick. Simple. Delicious. The broiler crisps the outer layer of fish while lemon zest enhances its natural mild flavor. Sometimes it's nice to allow the ingredients to speak for themselves.

Broiled Lemon Fish Fillets

pareve | passover | gluten-free | freezes well | yields 6 servings

Ingredients

6 fish fillets (e.g., sole, turbot, snapper, or pickerel) (about 6 oz/180 g each)

2 lemons, thinly sliced

kosher salt

freshly ground black pepper

1 tsp dried thyme or basil

1 Tbsp lemon zest

2 Tbsp lemon juice (preferably fresh)

1-2 Tbsp olive oil

Method

1. Adjust oven rack according to thickness of fish (see Norene's Notes, below). Preheat broiler. Line a rimmed baking sheet with parchment paper.

2. Place fish and lemon slices on prepared baking sheet. Sprinkle with salt, pepper, thyme, and lemon zest. Drizzle with lemon juice and olive oil.

3. Broil for 4-5 minutes (no turning required), or until fish flakes with a fork and lemon slices have browned.

4. Serve with lemon slices as garnish.

Norene's Notes

- Fish fillets at least ½-inch thick are best suited for broiling. The fish should be about 4 inches from the broiling element.
- Calculate 10 minutes per inch of thickness as your cooking time. If using frozen fish, calculate 20 minutes per inch of thickness.

This tangy pesto will enhance the subtle, sweet flavor of the fish. It's important to get the right sear on the fish when you're pan-frying — a crisp sear will keep the fish flaky and juicy.

Lemon-Spinach Pesto Fillets

dairy | passover | gluten-free | freezes well | yields 4-6 servings

Ingredients

Pesto

3 cups fresh spinach leaves

¾ cup fresh dill

3 cloves garlic
(about 1½ tsp minced)

1 tsp kosher salt

½ tsp black pepper

⅓ cup extra virgin olive oil

2 tsp lemon zest

¼ cup lemon juice
(preferably fresh)

¼ cup grated Parmesan cheese

Fish

1-2 Tbsp grapeseed or olive oil

4-6 halibut, sole, or tilapia fillets
(about 6 oz/180 g each)

kosher salt

freshly ground black pepper

Method

1. **Pesto:** Using a food processor or mini prep, process spinach, dill, garlic, salt, pepper, oil, lemon zest, and lemon juice until puréed. Add Parmesan; mix well.

2. **Fish:** In a large nonstick skillet, heat oil over medium-high heat. Season fillets generously with salt and pepper. Fry fillets 2-3 minutes per side, or until just cooked through.

3. Transfer fish to a platter and spoon pesto over fillets. Serve hot or at room temperature.

Norene's Notes

- Spinach and dill give this pesto a vibrant green color and fabulous flavor. Make a double batch of pesto and freeze half for another day. It thaws quickly, so you can prepare a gorgeous meal in under 10 minutes!
- Variation: If there are no nut allergies, add ¼ cup almonds when making the pesto. If you like more heat, add a dash or two of cayenne pepper or chili flakes.
- Leftover pesto is delicious mixed with rice or pasta.

So quick and easy, with a beautiful presentation, this is a terrific dish for weeknights or last-minute guests.

Baked Fish Fillets & Sautéed Mushrooms

pareve | passover | gluten-free | freezes well | yields 6 servings

Ingredients

Fish

6 sole, tilapia, or pickerel fillets (about 6 oz/180 g each)

1 Tbsp olive oil

1 tsp kosher salt

¼ tsp black pepper

2 tsp chopped fresh thyme leaves

Topping

2-3 Tbsp grapeseed oil

6 cups assorted mushrooms, roughly chopped

1 large onion, diced

¼ cup dry red wine

1 tsp chopped fresh thyme leaves

kosher salt

freshly ground black pepper

Method

1. Preheat oven to 375°F. Coat a 9 x 13-inch baking dish with nonstick cooking spray.

2. **Fish:** Brush fish on both sides with olive oil; season with salt, pepper, and thyme. Arrange in a single layer in baking dish. Bake, uncovered, for 10 minutes, or until fish flakes when lightly pressed with a fork.

3. **Topping:** Meanwhile, in a nonstick wok or skillet, heat oil over medium-high heat. Sauté mushrooms and onion for 7-8 minutes, or until golden and fragrant. Stir in wine and thyme. Bring to a simmer; cook 2-3 minutes longer. Season with salt and pepper to taste.

4. Spoon mushroom topping over fish before serving.

Norene's Notes

- Tilapia fillets have a thicker side and a thinner side. For more even cooking, cut each fillet in half lengthwise, making two long pieces. Cut the thicker piece in half crosswise. You will end up with three long pieces that are all about the same thickness.

- Thin fish fillets have a tendency to overcook when baked. To avoid this, fold each fillet in half so that the pointed tips meet, doubling up the thickness so that the fillets don't overcook.

My husband, Jeffery, grew up loving this meal. It's perfect for a weekend lunch or a weeknight dinner. Everyone loves to puncture the egg yolk and watch the runny yolk drip down over the fish and rice.

Tilapia & Rice
with sunny-side-up eggs

pareve | gluten-free option | do not freeze | yields 6 servings

Ingredients

1½ **cups** basmati rice (white or brown), rinsed and drained

6 tilapia fillets (about 6 oz/180 g each)

1 cup flour (regular or gluten-free) or corn starch

kosher salt

freshly ground black pepper

2 Tbsp grapeseed or vegetable oil

Topping

1 Tbsp grapeseed or vegetable oil

6 eggs

2 cups cherry tomatoes, halved

½ **cup** chopped fresh parsley

Method

1. Cook rice according to package directions. Meanwhile, prepare fish and topping.

2. **Fish:** Place flour into a shallow bowl. Sprinkle tilapia generously on both sides with salt and pepper. Dip into flour, coating both sides.

3. In a large skillet, heat oil over medium-high heat. Fry fish for 3-4 minutes per side, until golden. Transfer to a large plate and cover loosely with foil to keep warm.

4. **Topping:** In the same skillet, heat oil over low heat. Carefully slip eggs into skillet. Cook, covered, for 3-5 minutes or until whites are firm but yolks remain runny.

5. **Assembly:** Spoon rice onto individual plates, followed by cherry tomatoes and parsley. Top each serving with a fish fillet and a sunny-side-up egg. Serve immediately. Have each person puncture the egg yolk and stir gently to break the fish into chunks.

Norene's Notes

- Eggs-ellent: Covering the skillet with a lid when cooking eggs traps the heat and steam, cooking the eggs from above as well as below. A glass lid is ideal so you can check on the doneness of the eggs without uncovering them.

Poultry

For nutritional information on this section, see pages 323–324

Fried food isn't usually my thing, but this dish is irresistible. The chicken bites are perfectly crispy outside and tender inside. A hint of hot sauce kicks the sweet-and-sour duo into high gear for a flavor with serious zip and punch.

Sweet & Sour Chinese Chicken

meat | gluten-free | freezes well | yields 6 servings

Ingredients

6 single boneless skinless chicken breasts (or 12 boneless skinless thighs)

kosher salt

freshly ground black pepper

garlic powder

2 eggs

1 cup cornstarch or potato starch

oil, for frying

Sauce

½ cup ketchup

¼ cup honey

2 Tbsp soy sauce or tamari

2 Tbsp vinegar

6-8 drops hot sauce

2 scallions, thinly sliced, for garnish

Method

1. Cut chicken into 1-inch pieces. Sprinkle lightly on all sides with salt, pepper, and garlic powder.

2. Lightly beat eggs in a shallow bowl. Place cornstarch into second shallow bowl.

3. Dip chicken first into eggs, then into cornstarch, coating all sides.

4. In a large nonstick skillet, heat oil over medium-high heat. Working in batches, fry chicken on all sides until browned and crispy, cooked through, and juices run clear, 3-4 minutes per side.

5. Drain chicken on paper towels to absorb excess oil.

6. **Sauce:** In a saucepan, combine ketchup, honey, soy sauce, vinegar, and hot sauce. Bring to a boil over medium heat; then simmer for 2 minutes, stirring occasionally.

7. Transfer chicken to a serving platter; pour hot sauce over chicken. Garnish with sliced scallions.

Norene's Notes

- Chicken can be made ahead of time and kept warm in a 250°F oven. Add the sauce just before serving.
- For easy cleanup, put the cornstarch or potato starch into a resealable plastic bag. Add chicken pieces a few at a time and shake to coat. If you add too many pieces at a time, you'll end up with glue, not coating!

Fancy enough for company, easy enough for weeknights, this dish suits almost any occasion. It's those slow-simmered caramelized onions that keep me coming back to this dish, but the herb-seasoned chicken is juicy and delicious, too!

Grilled Chicken
with caramelized onions

meat | passover | gluten-free | freezes well | yields 6 servings

Ingredients

Caramelized Onions

2 Tbsp olive oil

4 onions, halved and thinly sliced

kosher salt

freshly ground black pepper

2 tsp chopped fresh thyme leaves (or your favorite herb)

Chicken

6 single boneless skinless chicken breasts (or 12 boneless skinless thighs)

kosher salt

freshly ground black pepper

3-4 cloves garlic, minced (about 2 tsp)

2 tsp chopped fresh thyme leaves (or your favorite herb)

1 Tbsp olive oil

Method

1. **Caramelized Onions:** Heat oil in a large skillet over medium-low heat. Add onions and cook for 25-30 minutes, until caramelized. Stir occasionally. Sprinkle with salt, pepper, and thyme. (Can be made ahead of time and reheated.)

2. **Chicken:** Rub chicken on both sides with salt, pepper, garlic, thyme, and oil. Marinate for a few minutes.

3. Preheat grill, setting it to medium-high. (See Norene's Notes, below.)

4. Grill chicken for 4-6 minutes per side, until grill marks appear and juices run clear.

5. Transfer chicken to a serving platter and smother with caramelized onions.

Norene's Notes

- No grill? Sauté the chicken in a nonstick skillet for 4-6 minutes per side, or bake it, uncovered, at 400°F for 20-25 minutes.
- Two-sided electric grills cook in half the time of a gas or charcoal grill. Chicken will be done in about 5 minutes, when it has reached 165°F on an instant-read thermometer.
- Quick clean-up: Place a moist soapy paper towel between the warm (not hot) grill plates. A few minutes later, the grill will wipe clean easily.

These amazing marinades will boost the flavor of your everyday chicken.

Beer-Marinated Chicken

meat | yields 6 servings

Ingredients

6 single boneless skinless chicken breasts (or 12 boneless skinless thighs)

kosher salt

freshly ground black pepper

1 tsp dried basil

1 tsp dried thyme

3 Tbsp olive oil

½ cup beer

3 cloves garlic, minced (about 1½ tsp)

Method

1. Sprinkle chicken on all sides with salt, pepper, basil, and thyme. Place chicken into a large resealable plastic bag. Add remaining ingredients. Seal bag tightly.

2. Marinate for 1-2 hours or overnight in the refrigerator, turning bag over occasionally so chicken is covered with marinade.

3. Remove chicken from refrigerator and let stand while preheating grill.

4. Remove chicken from marinade; discard marinade. Grill for 4-6 minutes per side, or until juices run clear.

Orange & Soy Marinated Chicken

meat | gluten-free | yields 6 servings

Ingredients

6 single boneless skinless chicken breasts (or 12 boneless skinless thighs)

kosher salt

freshly ground black pepper

2 tsp dried oregano

2 tsp orange zest

juice of **1** orange (about ¼ cup)

¼ cup olive oil

¼ cup soy sauce or tamari

2 tsp toasted sesame oil

2 Tbsp honey

4 cloves garlic, minced (about 2 tsp)

Method

1. Sprinkle chicken on all sides with salt, pepper, oregano, and orange zest. Place chicken into a large resealable plastic bag. Add remaining ingredients. Seal bag tightly.

2. Marinate for 1-2 hours or overnight in the refrigerator, turning bag over occasionally so chicken is covered with marinade.

3. Remove chicken from refrigerator and let stand while preheating grill.

4. Remove chicken from marinade; discard marinade. Grill for 4-6 minutes per side, or until juices run clear.

They are also excellent for fish or beef. These recipes all freeze well.

Basil-Marinated Chicken

meat | passover | gluten-free | yields 6 servings

Ingredients

6 single boneless skinless chicken breasts (or 12 boneless skinless thighs)

kosher salt

freshly ground black pepper

2 tsp onion powder

1 tsp sweet paprika

2 Tbsp olive oil

¼ cup red wine vinegar or balsamic vinegar

¼ cup chopped fresh basil

2 cloves garlic, minced (about 1 tsp)

Method

1. Sprinkle chicken on all sides with salt, pepper, onion powder, and paprika. Place chicken into a large resealable plastic bag. Add remaining ingredients. Seal bag tightly.

2. Marinate for 1-2 hours or overnight in the refrigerator, turning bag over occasionally so chicken is covered with marinade.

3. Remove chicken from refrigerator and let stand while preheating grill.

4. Remove chicken from marinade; discard marinade. Grill for 4-6 minutes per side, or until juices run clear.

Teriyaki Chicken

meat | gluten-free | yields 6 servings

Ingredients

6 single boneless skinless chicken breasts (or 12 boneless skinless thighs)

kosher salt

freshly ground black pepper

2 Tbsp olive oil

¼ cup honey

¼ cup soy sauce or tamari

juice of **1** lemon

4 cloves garlic, minced (about 2 tsp)

2 tsp chopped fresh ginger (optional)

Method

1. Sprinkle chicken on all sides with salt and pepper. Place chicken into a large resealable plastic bag. Add remaining ingredients. Seal bag tightly.

2. Marinate for 1-2 hours or overnight in the refrigerator, turning bag over occasionally so chicken is covered with marinade.

3. Remove chicken from refrigerator and let stand while preheating grill.

4. Remove chicken from marinade; discard marinade. Grill for 4-6 minutes per side, or until juices run clear.

Norene's Notes

- The marinade protects the chicken from forming harmful toxins that develop during grilling.
- No grill? Bake, uncovered, in a 400°F oven for about 25 minutes.

This easy, elegant salad will impress your guests with its bright tastes and summery colors. Layer the ingredients on small plates for an elegant appetizer or toss this salad family-style as a light course. This dish multiplies easily for a crowd.

Chicken, Mango & Avocado Salad

meat | gluten-free | do not freeze | yields 6 servings

Ingredients

4-6 single boneless skinless chicken breasts

1-2 Tbsp olive oil

kosher salt

freshly ground black pepper

2 Tbsp chopped fresh basil

6-8 cups mixed salad greens

½ red onion, thinly sliced

2 ripe mangoes, peeled and thinly sliced or cut into chunks

2 ripe avocados

Dressing

¼ cup rice vinegar

¼ cup lemon juice (preferably fresh)

½ cup extra virgin olive oil

2 Tbsp chopped fresh basil

½ tsp kosher salt, or to taste

freshly ground black pepper

Method

1. Preheat oven to 400°F. Coat a 9 x 13-inch baking dish with nonstick cooking spray.

2. Arrange chicken in a single layer in prepared baking dish. Drizzle with olive oil and sprinkle on both sides with salt, pepper, and basil.

3. Bake, uncovered, 20-25 minutes, or until chicken is cooked through and juices run clear. Let cool. (Can be prepared in advance and refrigerated.)

4. Dressing: Combine dressing ingredients in a glass jar, seal tightly, and shake well. Refrigerate until serving time.

5. Assembly: Place salad greens into a large serving bowl. Thinly slice each chicken breast across the grain or cut into bite-sized chunks. Arrange over greens.

6. Shortly before serving, pit and peel the avocados. Cut avocados into thin slices or chunks. Add onion, mangoes, and avocados to the salad. Drizzle with dressing. Serve chilled or at room temperature.

Norene's Notes

- Instead of baking the chicken, grill it about 5 minutes per side, until juices run clear.
- If preparing in advance, sprinkle cut avocado with lemon juice to prevent browning.

We've given traditional chicken schnitzel a food-trend twist by adding a sprinkling of healthy seeds. Flax and sesame give this dish a subtle nutty flavor and a superbly crunchy coating.

Three-Seeded Schnitzel

meat | gluten-free option | freezes well | yields 6 servings

Ingredients

6 boneless chicken breasts, pounded thin
(or 12 butterflied boneless skinless chicken thighs)

kosher salt

freshly ground black pepper

1 tsp sweet paprika

1½ cups panko crumbs
(regular or gluten-free)

¼ cup flax seeds

¼ cup white sesame seeds

¼ cup black sesame seeds

2 eggs

oil, for frying

1 lemon, cut into wedges, for garnish

Method

1. Sprinkle chicken on both sides with salt, pepper, and paprika.

2. Combine panko crumbs, flax seeds, and white and black sesame seeds in a medium bowl. Mix well. Lightly beat eggs in a second bowl.

3. Dip chicken first into egg, then into panko mixture, coating all sides.

4. In a large nonstick skillet, heat oil over medium-high heat. Working in batches, fry chicken on both sides until cooked through and juices run clear, 3-5 minutes per side.

5. Pat chicken with paper towel to remove excess oil. Keep warm in a 250°F oven or transfer to a serving platter. Garnish with lemon wedges.

Norene's Notes

- Flax seeds are extremely rich in soluble fiber and are an excellent source of omega-3 fatty acids; in order to access the omega-3s, flax seeds should be ground before using. An easy way to grind whole flax seeds is in a coffee grinder. For an extra fiber boost, add an additional 2-3 tablespoons of ground flax seeds to the panko mixture.

- To prevent flax seeds from becoming rancid, store them in the refrigerator or freezer.

One-pot dishes are essential for weeknight meals in my house. Known as the "long life" dish in the Philippines, this stir-fry, also called Pancit, is delicious and quick to prepare. Lots of vegetables and long noodles make for a long and happy life!

Rice Noodle Stir-Fry/Pancit

meat | gluten-free | do not freeze | yields 6-8 servings

Ingredients

6 single boneless skinless chicken breasts (or 12 boneless skinless thighs)

kosher salt

freshly ground black pepper

2 Tbsp grapeseed or vegetable oil

1 onion, halved and thinly sliced

2 stalks celery, thinly sliced

2 carrots, peeled and thinly sliced

2 red bell peppers, cut into chunks

1 cup snow peas, trimmed

4 cloves garlic, minced (about 2 tsp)

1 pkg (10 oz/300 g) thin rice noodles

⅓-½ **cup** soy sauce or tamari

1-2 tsp hot sauce

juice of ½ lemon

Method

1. Cut chicken into 2-inch pieces. Sprinkle with salt and pepper.

2. In a large nonstick wok or skillet, heat oil over medium-high heat. Sauté chicken for 3-5 minutes on each side, or until cooked through and juices run clear. Remove from wok.

3. Add onion, celery, carrots, bell peppers, snow peas, and garlic to wok; stir-fry until tender-crisp, 3-4 minutes.

4. Meanwhile, cook rice noodles according to package directions. They only take about 2 minutes to cook. Drain well. (If not using them immediately, cover with cold water and set aside. To reheat, place noodles into a colander and pour boiling water over them.)

5. Return chicken pieces to wok along with rice noodles, soy sauce, and hot sauce. Toss to combine.

6. Transfer to a serving platter. Drizzle with lemon juice.

Norene's Notes

- Instead of chicken, substitute 2 lb/1 kg thinly sliced beef. Instead of snow peas, add broccoli or cauliflower florets.
- No snow peas? Substitute frozen green peas or shelled edamame beans.

Making a dish as delicious as that of your local Chinese restaurant can be daunting, but here the bite-size chicken, garlicky soy, and tender button mushrooms reproduce the Chinese-takeout feeling. For true Chinese-fare flavor, serve over rice.

Chinese Chicken & Mushrooms

meat | gluten-free | freezes well | yields 6 servings

Ingredients

6 single boneless skinless chicken breasts (or 12 boneless skinless thighs)

4 cups button mushrooms, trimmed and halved

2 onions, thinly sliced

2 Tbsp vegetable oil

⅓ **cup** apricot preserves

¼ **cup** soy sauce or tamari

¼ **cup** rice vinegar

3 cloves garlic, minced (about 1½ tsp)

toasted sesame seeds, for garnish

sliced scallions, for garnish

Method

1. Cut chicken into 1-inch chunks. Place into a large resealable bag; add mushrooms and onions.

2. In a medium bowl, combine oil, preserves, soy sauce, rice vinegar, and garlic. Mix well. Add to chicken and seal bag tightly. Marinate for at least 20 minutes, or up to 24 hours in the refrigerator.

3. Carefully pour chicken, mushrooms, onions, and sauce into a large skillet. Bring to a boil; then reduce heat and simmer, uncovered, for 25 minutes. Stir occasionally.

4. Transfer to a large serving platter or bowl. Garnish with sesame seeds and scallions.

Norene's Notes

- Variation: Use 2 lb/1 kg stir-fry beef strips instead of chicken. Reduce cooking time to 18-20 minutes.
- It's in the bag! Omit mushrooms and onions. Combine chicken with marinade in a resealable freezer bag and store in the freezer. When needed, transfer the bag to the refrigerator and thaw overnight. Transfer the chicken and sauce to a skillet, add mushrooms and onions, and cook as directed. Ready when you are!

This unique combo of leeks, red pepper, and mango is perfect with roast chicken. The tropical taste of mango adds a sweet flavor and a pop of bright color. Be bold in the kitchen and try new things — that's the best way to cook.

Mango Chicken
with leeks & red peppers

meat | passover | gluten-free | freezes well | yields 8-10 servings

Ingredients

Chicken

2 chickens
(about 3 lb/1.4 kg each),
cut into eighths

kosher salt

freshly ground black pepper

2 tsp sweet paprika

2 tsp onion powder

2 tsp garlic powder

2 tsp dried basil

¼ cup honey

Topping

2 Tbsp olive oil

3 large leeks, thinly sliced
(see Norene's Notes, below)

2 red bell peppers,
halved and thinly sliced

2 mangoes,
peeled and thinly sliced

½ tsp kosher salt, or to taste

freshly ground black pepper

Method

1. Preheat oven to 400°F. Coat a large roasting pan with nonstick cooking spray.

2. Trim and discard excess fat from chicken pieces. Arrange chicken, skin side up, in a single layer in prepared pan. Sprinkle with salt, pepper, paprika, onion powder, garlic powder, and basil. Drizzle honey over chicken. Rub chicken on all sides to coat with spices and honey. (Can be prepared up to 24 hours in advance and refrigerated, covered.)

3. Roast, uncovered, for 1 hour and 20 minutes, until cooked through and juices run clear. Baste occasionally.

4. **Topping:** Meanwhile, in a large wok or skillet, heat oil over medium-high heat. Sauté leeks and red peppers for 7-8 minutes, until golden. Stir in mangoes. Season with salt and pepper; cook until heated through, about 3 minutes.

5. Transfer chicken to a serving platter; pour on topping.

Norene's Notes

• To clean leeks, trim off most of the green part of each leek. Make 4 lengthwise cuts almost to the root so that the leek resembles a broom. Swish leeks in a sink filled with cold water to remove any sand or grit. Dry well. Cut off and discard root end.

• Shortcut: Substitute 2 cups frozen mango chunks. No need to thaw first — just add an extra minute to the cooking time so they are heated through.

This easy, one-pot meal puts a new twist on an old classic. Everyone loves roast chicken with onions, so why not sweeten the deal with a little honey? Simple and delicious.

Honey-Roasted Chicken
with squash & onions

meat | passover | gluten-free | freezes well | yields 4-6 servings

Ingredients

1 chicken (about 3 lb/1.4 kg), cut into eighths

2 onions, cut into chunks

4 cups butternut squash chunks (see Norene's Notes, below)

kosher salt

freshly ground black pepper

1 tsp sweet paprika

¼ tsp chili powder (or to taste)

3 cloves garlic, minced (about 1½ tsp)

1 tsp dried tarragon or thyme

½ cup honey

½ cup water or chicken broth

Method

1. Preheat oven to 400°F. Coat a large roasting pan with nonstick cooking spray.

2. Trim and discard excess fat from chicken pieces. Arrange chicken, skin side up, in prepared pan. Add onions and squash, tucking them between chicken pieces.

3. Sprinkle with salt, pepper, paprika, chili powder, garlic, and tarragon. Drizzle with honey; rub to coat chicken and vegetables on all sides. Add water to baking dish.

4. Roast, uncovered, for 1 hour and 20 minutes, until glazed and golden. Baste occasionally. If necessary, drizzle in a little additional water.

Norene's Notes

- Use local honey when possible. When you eat honey that's produced where you live, you become desensitized to the local pollens, which helps prevent allergies and hay fever.
- Butternut squash chunks are sold in packages, which can save you time and energy.
- See Sweet Potato & Squash Soup (p. 54) for tips on cutting butternut squash more easily.

In this delicious family favorite, the chicken absorbs the bold, tangy flavor of the sun-dried tomatoes and is perfectly complemented by the aromatic fresh basil. It's beautiful to serve and even easier to make. This recipe multiplies well.

Basil Chicken
with sun-dried tomatoes

meat | passover | gluten-free | freezes well | yields 4-6 servings

Ingredients

1 chicken (about 3 lb/1.4 kg), cut into eighths

kosher salt

freshly ground black pepper

1 cup sun-dried tomatoes, thinly sliced (see Norene's Notes, below)

3-4 cloves garlic, minced (about 2 tsp)

1 cup fresh basil leaves, coarsely chopped (see Norene's Notes, below)

3 Tbsp olive oil

additional sun-dried tomatoes and basil, for garnish

Method

1. Preheat oven to 375°F. Coat a 9 x 13-inch baking dish with nonstick cooking spray.

2. Trim and discard excess fat from chicken pieces. Arrange in a single layer, skin side up, in baking dish; sprinkle with salt and pepper on all sides.

3. In a medium bowl, combine sun dried-tomatoes, garlic, basil, and oil. Mix well. Spread evenly over chicken.

4. Roast, uncovered, for 1 hour and 20 minutes, or until cooked through and juices run clear. Baste occasionally.

5. Garnish with additional sun-dried tomatoes and basil.

Norene's Notes

- If you use oil-packed sun-dried tomatoes, drain and rinse them well. If the tomatoes you are using are not packed in oil, soak them briefly in hot water to rehydrate them first.

- If fresh basil is too expensive or hard to find, use a combination of equal parts fresh basil and baby spinach or flat-leaf parsley.

Simple and rustic, with the classic flavors of fresh herbs, lemon, and garlic, this dish is a perfect example of simple elegance. The lemon adds a burst of flavor that you can taste in every bite. It's a great dish to serve to company.

Lemon-Herb Chicken
with roasted garlic

meat | passover | gluten-free | freezes well | yields 4-6 servings

Ingredients

1 chicken
(about 3 lb/1.4 kg),
cut into eighths

kosher salt

freshly ground black pepper

¼ cup chopped fresh parsley

¼ cup chopped fresh dill

2 Tbsp minced fresh rosemary

12-15 cloves garlic, peeled
(about 1 head)

¼ cup olive oil

juice of **1** lemon
(about 3-4 Tbsp)

2 Tbsp honey

additional herbs, for garnish

Method

1. Preheat oven to 375°F. Coat a 9 x 13-inch baking dish with nonstick cooking spray.

2. Trim and discard excess fat from chicken pieces. Arrange chicken, skin side up, in a single layer in prepared dish. Sprinkle with salt and pepper on all sides.

3. In a medium bowl, combine parsley, dill, rosemary, whole garlic cloves, oil, lemon juice, and honey. Mix well. Drizzle evenly over chicken.

4. Bake, covered, for 1 hour. Uncover and bake for 20-25 minutes more, until glazed and golden. Baste occasionally.

5. Transfer to a platter; garnish with additional fresh herbs.

Norene's Notes

- Garlic cloves become sweet and mellow when roasted. You can often buy garlic cloves that are already peeled. Leftover roasted garlic is fabulous when spread on toasted bread, especially challah!

- To peel garlic easily, place a head of garlic on a cutting board and cover with a dishtowel. Firmly hit the towel-covered garlic with the bottom of a heavy skillet. Remove the towel, separate the cloves, and pick out the papery skins. Repeat several times if necessary, discarding any remaining skins.

- Variation: To make this into a musical dish, add 1 Tbsp chopped thyme leaves. You'll have them singing for their supper.

Enticingly aromatic, this baked chicken recipe is a quick, easy way to bring a dash of curry to your kitchen. It's a 3-layer flavor sensation of crunch, punch, and candy.

Candied Curry Chicken

meat | gluten-free option | freezes well | yields 4-6 servings

Ingredients

1 egg

4 cups cornflakes
(regular or gluten-free)
(see Norene's Notes, below)

1 chicken
(about 3 lb/1.4 kg),
cut into eighths

1 tsp curry powder

1 tsp sweet paprika

1 tsp turmeric

1 tsp garlic powder

3-4 Tbsp brown sugar

1 tsp kosher salt

¼ tsp black pepper

juice of **1** lemon
(about 3-4 Tbsp)

Method

1. Preheat oven to 375°F. Line a rimmed baking sheet with parchment paper.

2. In a medium bowl, lightly beat egg. Place cornflakes into a resealable bag; seal tightly. Coarsely crush cornflakes with your hands or a rolling pin.

3. Trim and discard excess fat from chicken pieces. Remove and discard skin. Dip chicken pieces into egg, then drop them into crumbs, a few at a time, shaking the bag to coat all sides.

4. Arrange chicken pieces, skin side up, in a single layer on prepared pan. Bake, uncovered, for 30 minutes.

5. Meanwhile, in a small bowl, combine curry powder, paprika, turmeric, garlic powder, brown sugar, salt, pepper, and lemon juice. Mix well.

6. Spoon mixture evenly over chicken. Bake 30 minutes longer, until chicken pieces are glazed and golden.

Norene's Notes

• This recipe works well with chicken wings or drumsticks.
• Short Cut: Use 1 cup cornflake crumbs (regular or gluten-free) instead of crushing the cornflakes yourself.
• Each curry blend can include a different blend of spices in varying amounts, ranging from sweet to hot, making each curry powder unique.

The Asian ingredients for this mouthwatering dish are available in any supermarket. Fresh ginger adds a spicy-sweet flavor.

Sesame-Ginger Chicken

meat | gluten-free | freezes well | yields 4-6 servings

Ingredients

1 chicken (about 3 lb/1.4 kg), cut into eighths

¼ cup soy sauce or tamari

¼ cup brown sugar, lightly packed

¼ cup ketchup

4 cloves garlic, minced (about 2 tsp)

2 tsp minced fresh ginger

1 tsp toasted sesame oil (optional)

2 Tbsp sesame seeds

sliced scallions, for garnish

Method

1. Preheat oven to 375°F. Coat a 9 x 13-inch baking dish with nonstick cooking spray.

2. Trim and discard excess fat from chicken pieces. Remove skin, if desired. Arrange chicken in a single layer in prepared dish.

3. In a medium bowl, combine soy sauce, brown sugar, ketchup, garlic, ginger, and sesame oil, if using. Mix well.

4. Using a pastry brush, coat chicken with half of marinade; reserve remaining marinade.

5. Bake, covered, for 45 minutes. Coat chicken with remaining marinade; sprinkle with sesame seeds. Bake, uncovered, 30 minutes longer, until glazed and golden.

6. Transfer to a serving platter; garnish with scallions.

Norene's Notes

• Store fresh ginger in the freezer. When needed, just grate as much as you need — no thawing required. Ginger keeps about 6 months in the freezer.

We all need wow dishes in our culinary repertoire, especially when hosting a holiday or celebratory feast. This dish reminds us of home and celebrations; most importantly, it reminds us that food should be enjoyed with family and friends.

Rolled Turkey Roast
with deli strips

meat | passover option | gluten-free | freezes well | yields 8 servings

Ingredients

1 boneless, skinless rolled turkey breast or roast (about 4 lb/1.8 kg)

kosher salt

freshly ground black pepper

2 tsp dried thyme

¾ cup ketchup

½ cup brown sugar, packed

1 Tbsp Dijon mustard

2 Tbsp vinegar

¾ lb/375 g sliced deli meat (corned beef, pastrami, or smoked meat)

½ cup water

Method

1. Coat a large, heavy roasting pan with nonstick cooking spray.

2. Place turkey into prepared pan. Sprinkle on all sides with salt, pepper, and thyme.

3. In a medium bowl, combine ketchup, brown sugar, mustard, and vinegar. Mix well to make a sauce.

4. Pour half the sauce over the turkey, coating it on all sides.

5. Lay deli slices over turkey, covering it completely. Pour on remaining sauce. Spread sauce all over without moving the deli slices. (Can be prepared several hours ahead of time and refrigerated.)

6. Preheat oven to 350°F. Pour water into bottom of roasting pan. Cover pan loosely with foil. Roast, covered, for about 1¼-1½ hours.

7. Uncover and roast 30 minutes longer, basting occasionally. Calculate 25-30 minutes per pound to determine total cooking time.

8. Let turkey stand for 15-20 minutes. Slice turkey (an electric knife makes it easier). Transfer to serving platter; serve with pan juices.

Norene's Notes

- When roast is done, a meat thermometer should register an internal temperature of 165-170°F.
- Allow 6 hours per pound for frozen turkey to thaw in the refrigerator. A rolled turkey breast or roast will take about 1 day; a whole turkey will take 2-3 days.
- Passover Option: Omit vinegar and Dijon mustard or use Passover imitation mustard.

Meat

For nutritional information on this section, see pages 324–325

Skirt steak is easy to marinate and quick to prepare, making it a perfect weeknight choice. The meat is tender and juicy on the inside, with a crispy sear on the outside. For guests, I serve thin slices of steak over salad greens.

Marinated Skirt Steak

meat | gluten-free | freezes well | yields 4-6 servings

Ingredients

1 skirt steak (about 2 lb/1 kg)

¼ cup soy sauce or tamari

¼ cup balsamic vinegar

2 Tbsp honey

2 Tbsp lime juice (preferably fresh)

2 cloves garlic, minced (about 1 tsp)

2 tsp minced fresh rosemary or thyme

freshly ground black pepper

Method

1. Place steak into a large resealable plastic bag; add soy sauce, balsamic vinegar, honey, lime juice, garlic, rosemary, and pepper. Seal bag tightly.

2. Marinate for 1 hour or up to 24 hours in the refrigerator. Turn bag over occasionally so meat is covered with marinade.

3. Remove from refrigerator and let stand while preheating broiler or grill. If broiling, spray broiling rack with nonstick spray and line bottom tray with foil.

4. Remove steak from marinade; discard marinade. Broil or grill for 4-6 minutes per side or until meat reaches desired doneness. (For medium, cook to 145°F.)

5. Let steak rest for 5 minutes for easier slicing. Slice against the grain into thin slices.

Norene's Notes

• Skirt steak is marbled with fat and is tender and juicy. It comes from the beef plate, the underside of the animal below the ribs. Grill or broil skirt steak quickly over high heat for best results.

• Leftovers are great in grilled sandwiches or stir-fries.

I created this recipe one Sunday afternoon while scouring the pantry for dinner ingredients and ideas. This serves up beautifully and is one of my absolute favorite dishes. In the summer, it's great on the grill.

Raspberry London Broil

meat | passover | gluten-free | freezes well | yields 6 servings

Ingredients

1 London broil (about 2 lb/1.8 kg)

1 tsp kosher salt

freshly ground black pepper

1 tsp dried thyme

2 cloves garlic, minced (about 1 tsp)

⅔ cup raspberry jam

⅔ cup barbecue sauce

1 tsp lemon juice (preferably fresh)

Method

1. Sprinkle meat with salt, pepper, thyme, and garlic. Rub to coat on all sides.

2. Preheat broiler or grill. If broiling, spray broiling rack with nonstick spray and line bottom tray with foil.

3. Broil or grill for 8-10 minutes per side or until meat reaches desired doneness. (For medium, cook to 145°F.)

4. Meanwhile, in a small saucepan, combine jam, barbecue sauce, and lemon juice. Bring to a boil over medium heat. Reduce heat and simmer for 2 minutes, stirring once or twice.

5. Let meat rest for 5 minutes. Slice against the grain, on the diagonal, into thin slices.

6. Transfer to a serving platter. Pour heated sauce over meat.

Norene's Notes

- Variation: Serve sliced meat in warm corn tortillas. Top with chopped jalapeños, onions, cilantro, and raspberry sauce.

Although I'm not much of a coffee drinker, the dark, bold flavors of this dish are really enticing. This quick, easy dish is perfect for hosting guests. Sophistication on a plate!

Coffee-Rubbed London Broil

meat | passover | gluten-free | freezes well | yields 10-12 servings

Ingredients

Spice Rub

1 Tbsp instant coffee granules

1 Tbsp brown sugar

1 Tbsp sweet paprika

1 tsp chili powder (or to taste)

1 tsp kosher salt

¼ tsp black pepper

1 tsp garlic powder

1 tsp onion powder

1 tsp dried oregano

1 tsp unsweetened cocoa powder

Meat

2 London broils (each about 2 lb/1.8 kg)

⅔ cup barbecue sauce

Method

1. **Spice rub:** Combine ingredients for spice rub in a large resealable bag.

2. Add meat to the bag and rub on all sides with spice rub. Marinate in the refrigerator for at least 1 hour or up to 24 hours.

3. Remove meat from refrigerator and let stand while preheating broiler or grill. If broiling, spray broiling pan with nonstick cooking spray and line bottom tray with foil.

4. Transfer meat to prepared pan; spread barbecue sauce over the top. Broil or grill for 8-10 minutes per side or until meat reaches desired doneness. (For medium, cook to 145°F.)

5. Let meat rest for 5 minutes. Slice against the grain, on the diagonal, into thin slices. Transfer to a serving platter. Serve hot or cold.

Norene's Notes

- You can make several batches of this scrumptious spice rub and store it in the pantry. Each batch makes about ⅓ cup. Ready when you are!
- For a smaller group, make only half the recipe, using one London broil.
- Leftovers are great added to a salad the next day.

This crowd-pleaser can be made mild to very hot, depending on how much jalapeño you use. Remember not to touch your eyes after chopping! Roast ribs until they are tender, succulent, fall-off-the-bone good. They taste best when made the day before.

Jalapeño Short Ribs

meat | passover | gluten-free | freezes well | yields 6-8 servings

Ingredients

Spice Rub

¼ cup brown sugar, lightly packed

1 tsp chili flakes (or to taste)

2 tsp kosher salt (or to taste)

1 tsp black pepper

3 Tbsp sweet paprika

1 Tbsp garlic powder

1 Tbsp onion powder

Meat

8 beef short ribs (flanken) (about 6 lb/2.7 kg)

2 cups tomato sauce

⅓ cup brown sugar, lightly packed

¼ cup lemon juice (preferably fresh)

1 tsp dried basil

2-3 jalapeño peppers, finely chopped (remove seeds for less heat)

Method

1. **Spice rub:** In a medium bowl, combine ingredients for spice rub; mix well.

2. Coat a large roasting pan with nonstick cooking spray.

3. Arrange short ribs in a single layer in prepared roasting pan. Season ribs on all sides with spice rub. Let stand for 20-30 minutes.

4. Preheat oven to 400°F. Roast, uncovered, for 30 minutes. Drain and discard fat. Reduce oven temperature to 325°F.

5. In a medium bowl, combine tomato sauce, brown sugar, lemon juice, basil, and jalapeños. Mix well. Pour over, around, and under meat.

6. Cover pan tightly with foil and cook for 3 hours, until fork-tender. Baste occasionally.

Norene's Notes

- What's Your Beef? Short ribs (flanken) are ¾-1-inch thick and are the easiest to find. English ribs are double the thickness of regular flanken, so there is more meat to eat. Miami ribs are long, thin strips (about ½-inch thick) and cook more quickly than regular flanken.

- Variation: This recipe also works well with brisket, top rib, or second-cut fillet roast. Season meat on all sides with spice rub, then top with sauce mixture. Roast, covered, at 325°F, calculating 45 minutes per pound.

Sweet, sticky, and succulent, honeyed spare ribs are the quintessential finger-licking dish. This simple recipe is a year-round favorite that has saved me on many occasions. The scrumptious sauce is also great for pot roast and chicken.

Sticky Miami Ribs

meat | gluten-free | freezes well | yields 6 servings

Ingredients

12 Miami beef ribs

⅓ cup ketchup

⅓ cup soy sauce or tamari

⅓ cup orange juice

3 Tbsp honey

4 cloves garlic, minced (about 2 tsp)

2 tsp minced ginger (optional)

2 scallions, thinly sliced, for garnish

Method

1. Preheat oven to 350°F. Coat a large roasting pan with nonstick cooking spray.

2. Arrange ribs in a single layer in prepared pan.

3. In a small bowl, whisk together ketchup, soy sauce, orange juice, honey, garlic, and ginger, if using. Pour mixture over ribs.

4. Cover and marinate for 1 hour or up to 24 hours in the refrigerator.

5. Bake, covered, about 1½-2 hours, or until meat is tender. Baste occasionally.

6. Garnish with sliced scallions.

Norene's Notes

- Miami ribs are a thin-cut version of short ribs (flanken). Regular flanken can be substituted; cooking time will be about 3 hours.
- Variation: Omit orange juice; use pure maple syrup instead of honey. Drain juice from 1 can (14 oz/398 ml) pineapple chunks; add ⅓ cup juice to sauce mixture. Add pineapple chunks to ribs during the last 20-30 minutes of baking.

Whether served as a mouth-watering starter or a succulent main dish, these maple-smothered ribs are delicious on any dinner menu. From casual to sophisticated, this dish caters to all occasions, and the finger-licking-good glaze kicks it up a notch.

Maple-Mustard Miami Ribs

meat | passover option | gluten-free | freezes well | yields 4-6 servings

Ingredients

12 Miami beef ribs, (see Norene's Notes, p. 152) cut into individual ribs

1 medium onion, sliced into rings

kosher salt

freshly ground black pepper

1 tsp sweet paprika

¼ cup Dijon mustard

½ cup pure maple syrup

1 Tbsp balsamic vinegar

water, as needed

Method

1. Coat a 9 x 13-inch baking dish with nonstick spray.

2. Arrange ribs in a single layer in prepared baking dish; top with onion rings. Sprinkle with salt, pepper, and paprika.

3. In a small bowl, whisk together Dijon mustard, maple syrup, and balsamic vinegar. Spread mixture over ribs.

4. Cover and marinate for 1 hour or up to 24 hours in the refrigerator.

5. Preheat oven to 350°F.

6. Bake, covered, about 1½ hours or until meat is almost tender. Uncover and bake an additional 20 minutes, basting occasionally. If necessary, stir in a little water.

7. Serve on individual plates or on a large serving platter.

Norene's Notes

• Mustard loses its pungency over time, so for maximum flavor store it either in a cool dark place or in the refrigerator.

• Passover Option: Use honey and imitation mustard for Passover.

Prime rib is the ultimate beef cut, and the ultimate way to prepare it is to marinate it in bourbon. When I'm cooking for a celebration, this is what I make. It's a winner!

Bourbon Marinated Prime Rib

meat | gluten-free option | leftovers freeze well | yields 6 servings

Ingredients

1 standing rib roast (about 4 lb/1.8 kg)

kosher salt

freshly ground black pepper

4 cloves garlic, minced (about 2 tsp)

½ cup bourbon

¼ cup honey

¼ cup soy sauce or tamari

Method

1. Sprinkle meat with salt, pepper, and garlic. Rub to coat on all sides. Place into a large resealable plastic bag.

2. Add bourbon, honey, and soy sauce; seal bag tightly. Work in marinade by massaging it into meat. Let marinate in the refrigerator for 2 hours or up to 24 hours, turning occasionally.

3. Remove meat from refrigerator and bring to room temperature. Preheat oven to 450°F. Coat a roasting pan with nonstick cooking spray.

4. Remove roast from marinade and place into prepared pan, rib side down. Discard marinade.

5. Roast, uncovered, for 25 minutes. Reduce heat to 325°F.

6. For medium, roast an additional 18-20 minutes per lb (about 1¼ hours). For well-done, roast an additional 25 minutes per lb (about 1⅔ hours).

7. Transfer meat to a cutting board and tent loosely with foil. Let meat rest for about 15 minutes before carving.

8. Using a sharp carving knife, slice across the grain.

Norene's Notes

• An easy way to order a standing rib roast is by the number of ribs. Calculate 1 rib per person, plus extra for second helpings.

• For easier carving, ask your butcher to cut meat off the bone and then retie the ribs.

• Putting a pan of water on the lower rack when roasting helps reduce shrinkage.

Long, slow cooking and marinating are the secrets to a delicious brisket. Within an hour of my beginning to cook this dish, the house has a wonderful, inviting aroma. My family can hardly wait for dinner!

Balsamic-Braised Brisket

meat | passover | gluten-free | freezes well | yields 8-10 servings

Ingredients

1 beef brisket (4-5 lb /1.8-2.3 kg)

2 tsp kosher salt

1 tsp black pepper

1 Tbsp onion powder

1 Tbsp garlic powder

2 Tbsp olive oil

3 large onions, thinly sliced

¼ cup chopped fresh parsley

1 can (6 oz/170 g) tomato paste

2 Tbsp honey

3 bay leaves

½ cup balsamic vinegar

¾ cup dry red wine or water

Method

1. Coat a large roasting pan with nonstick cooking spray. Add brisket; sprinkle with salt, pepper, onion powder, and garlic powder. Rub brisket with spices to coat on all sides.

2. In a large nonstick skillet, heat oil over medium heat. Sauté onions for 5 minutes, until softened. Stir in parsley, tomato paste, honey, bay leaves, vinegar, and wine. Simmer for 5 minutes, stirring occasionally. Let cool.

3. Pour sauce over, around, and under the brisket. Cover and marinate in the refrigerator for at least 1 hour or overnight, turning occasionally.

4. Preheat oven to 325°F. Bake, covered, for 3-3½ hours or until meat is fork-tender. Calculate 45 minutes per pound to determine the cooking time. Discard bay leaves. Let cool.

5. Refrigerate several hours or overnight. Discard hardened fat from gravy. Trim excess fat from brisket. Slice against the grain to desired thickness.

6. Reheat, covered, in pan gravy at 350°F for 25-30 minutes.

Norene's Notes

• Slow Cooker Method: Season brisket and prepare sauce as above; add to slow cooker insert coated with nonstick cooking spray. Marinate overnight in the refrigerator. Place insert into slow cooker; cook on on low for 8-10 hours.

• Ask your butcher to cut a very large brisket (8 lb/3.6 kg) in half. Total cooking time will be the same as for one 4 lb/1.8 kg brisket.

• Brisket should be cooked "low and slow," with lots of onions. The internal temperature should not rise above 180°F on a meat thermometer; after it reaches 200°F, the brisket will become dry.

The onions and ketchup tenderize this easy, no-fail brisket, creating a melt-in-your-mouth flavor. I often use this for Shabbat lunch; after cooking it thoroughly, I keep it in the oven overnight at 225°F. It's tender and delicious by morning.

Best Roast Brisket

meat | gluten-free | freezes well | yields 10-12 servings

Ingredients

1 beef brisket
(about 5-6 lb/2.3-2.7 kg)

4 medium onions, chopped

2-3 tsp kosher salt

1 tsp black pepper

2 tsp dried basil

4 cloves garlic, minced
(about 2 tsp)

¾ cup ketchup

¼ cup soy sauce or tamari

2 Tbsp lemon juice

½ cup brown sugar,
lightly packed

2 tsp hot sauce

½ cup water or dry red wine

Method

1. Place brisket and onions into a large roasting pan coated with nonstick cooking spray. Sprinkle brisket with salt, pepper, basil, and garlic. Rub to coat on all sides.

2. Make a sauce by combining ketchup, soy sauce, lemon juice, brown sugar, hot sauce, and water in a medium bowl. Mix well.

3. Pour sauce over, around, and under the brisket and onions. Cover and refrigerate for 1 hour or overnight.

4. Preheat oven to 325°F.

5. Bake, covered, for 3½-4 hours or until meat is fork-tender. Calculate 45 minutes per pound to determine the cooking time.

6. Let cool. Refrigerate for several hours or overnight.

7. Remove and discard hardened fat from gravy. Trim excess fat from brisket. Slice against the grain to desired thickness.

8. Reheat, covered, in pan gravy at 350°F for 25-30 minutes.

Norene's Notes

• A single brisket (first cut) is leaner and less tender than a double brisket (second cut), which has a thick layer of fat sandwiched between the two sections.

• Slow Cooker Method: Season brisket and prepare sauce as directed above. Combine brisket and sauce in slow cooker insert coated with nonstick cooking spray. Marinate overnight in the refrigerator. Place insert into slow cooker; cook on low for 10-12 hours.

This dish presents beautifully and tastes amazing. The tangy sweet sauce complements the saltiness of the beef. There's always an occasion to serve a bright and festive dish — and if there isn't, make one!

Cranberry-Glazed Corned Beef

meat | passover option | gluten-free | freezes well | yields 8 servings

Ingredients

1 or 2 pickled briskets (about 4 lb/1.8 kg total)

1 can (14 oz/397 g) jellied or whole berry cranberry sauce

¼ cup soy sauce or tamari

1 Tbsp lemon juice (preferably fresh)

2 cloves garlic, minced (about 1 tsp)

Method

1. Bring a large pot of water to a boil. Add meat and simmer, partially covered, for 2½ hours, or until fork tender. Drain and let cool. (Can be made up to a day in advance and refrigerated.)

2. Make a sauce by stirring together cranberry sauce, soy sauce, lemon juice, and garlic in a medium bowl.

3. Preheat oven to 350°F. Coat a 9 x 13-inch baking dish with nonstick cooking spray.

4. Slice meat across the grain into thin slices. Transfer to prepared baking dish and pour sauce over.

5. Cover and bake for 30 minutes, until glazed and bubbly.

Norene's Notes

- Butchers often use smaller briskets for their corned beef. If you use smaller ones, reduce boiling time slightly.
- To reduce the saltiness of corned beef, soak it in cold water for 30 minutes before cooking. Drain well and cook in fresh water.
- Passover Option: Replace soy sauce with ketchup or balsamic vinegar.

If you love tongue, you'll love this dish with its sweet and tangy sauce, inspired by my Bubbie, Mena Glustein. I like to make this for my husband, Jeffery, and our more adventurous dinner guests, especially for the High Holidays.

Sweet & Tangy Pickled Tongue

meat | passover option | gluten-free | freezes well | yields 6 servings

Ingredients

1 pickled beef tongue (about 3 lb/1.2 kg)

½ cup brown sugar, lightly packed

¼ cup ketchup

1 tsp Dijon mustard

2 Tbsp vinegar or lemon juice

½ cup raisins (optional)

Method

1. Bring a large pot of water to a boil. Add tongue and simmer, covered, for 2½ hours, or until fork tender.

2. Drain well. Immediately immerse tongue in a large bowl of cold water. Peel off and discard skin, small bones, and gristle. (Tongue can be prepared to this point up to a day in advance; cover and refrigerate.)

3. In a medium bowl, make a sauce by stirring together brown sugar, ketchup, mustard, vinegar, and raisins, if using.

4. Preheat oven to 350°F. Spray a 9 x 13-inch baking dish with nonstick cooking spray.

5. Slice tongue crosswise into thin slices. Transfer to prepared baking dish; pour sauce over meat.

6. Cover and bake for 30 minutes.

Norene's Notes

- Variation: Use pickled brisket instead of tongue; cooking instructions remain the same.
- Passover Option: Use either Passover imitation mustard or white horseradish.

This is an easy way to serve nutrient-rich greens. Substitute baby bok choy, Swiss chard, or spinach for kale. Serve the juicy, tender beef, with its bright, gingery flavor, over rice, rice noodles, quinoa, or even spaghetti squash!

Beef Stir-Fry
with kale & peppers

meat | gluten-free | do not freeze | yields 6 servings

Ingredients

2 lb/1 kg beef stir-fry (pepper steak)

4 Tbsp grapeseed or olive oil, divided

2 Tbsp lemon juice (preferably fresh)

4 cloves garlic, minced (about 2 tsp)

2 tsp minced fresh ginger

kosher salt

freshly ground black pepper

1 large onion, halved and thinly sliced

1 red bell pepper, halved and thinly sliced

1 orange bell pepper, halved and thinly sliced

1 yellow bell pepper, halved and thinly sliced

½ cup soy sauce or tamari

1 Tbsp toasted sesame oil (optional)

2 Tbsp cornstarch dissolved in **¼ cup** orange juice

1 bunch kale, stems and tough ribs discarded

Method

1. Place beef into a large bowl. Add 2 tablespoons oil, lemon juice, garlic, ginger, salt, and pepper. Mix well. Marinate for 30 minutes. Drain well, reserving marinade.

2. Heat remaining 2 tablespoons oil in a nonstick wok or skillet over medium-high heat. Pat beef dry with paper towels to prevent spatters. Stir-fry beef for 4-5 minutes, until lightly browned.

3. Add onion and peppers; stir-fry 3-4 minutes longer.

4. Add reserved marinade, soy sauce, and sesame oil, if using. Heat until simmering.

5. Stir in cornstarch mixture; cook 1-2 minutes, until bubbling and thickened.

6. Tear kale leaves into pieces; add to skillet. Cook 2 minutes longer, stirring often, just until heated through. Serve immediately.

Norene's Notes

• Your food processor will slice the vegetables in moments.

• Chicken Stir-Fry: Substitute thinly sliced chicken strips for beef. If desired, substitute ¼ cup hoisin sauce for soy sauce or tamari.

• Freeze leftover ginger. It grates easily while still frozen.

Lamb chops are always elegant and deceptively easy to prepare. All the prep work can be done the day before. Garnished with lemon and lime slices, this beautiful dish will impress your family.

Lemon-Lime Lamb Chops

meat | passover | gluten-free | freezes well | yields 4 servings

Ingredients

8 first-cut lamb chops

kosher salt

freshly ground black pepper

2 cloves garlic, minced (about 1 tsp)

½ tsp sweet paprika

½ tsp dried rosemary or thyme

juice of **1** lemon (about 3 Tbsp)

juice of **1** lime (about 2 Tbsp)

1 Tbsp olive oil

1 lemon, thinly sliced

1 lime, thinly sliced

Method

1. Sprinkle lamb chops on both sides with salt, pepper, garlic, paprika, and rosemary.

2. Place into a resealable plastic bag; add lemon juice, lime juice, and olive oil. Seal tightly. Marinate for 2 hours or up to 24 hours in the refrigerator, turning bag over occasionally.

3. Remove meat from refrigerator and bring to room temperature.

4. Preheat broiler or grill. If broiling, spray broiling rack with nonstick spray and line bottom tray with foil.

5. Remove lamb chops from marinade; discard marinade. Broil or grill chops for 4-6 minutes per side or until meat reaches desired doneness. (For medium, cook to 145°F.)

6. While lamb is grilling, grill lemon and lime slices for 3-4 minutes per side, until grill marks appear.

7. Transfer meat to a serving platter and garnish with grilled lemon and lime slices.

Norene's Notes

- Marinating meat, poultry, and fish in an acid-based marinade before grilling greatly reduces the formation of HCA's (heterocyclic amines), the harmful toxins created when grilling foods over high temperatures.

- A resealable plastic bag is an excellent container to use for marinating since the food is coated with the marinade more evenly than in a baking pan.

This dish originated in the Mediterranean region, where stuffed vegetables are a staple. One bite of this intensely flavorful dish and you'll understand why. It's great as a main course or as an appetizer when hosting a group.

Stuffed Eggplant

meat | gluten-free | do not freeze | yields 6 servings

Ingredients

Eggplant

3 medium eggplants, halved lengthwise

2 Tbsp olive oil

kosher salt

freshly ground black pepper

Meat

2 Tbsp olive oil

1 large onion, diced

4 cloves garlic, minced (about 2 tsp)

1 lb/500 g lean ground beef (or ground veal, chicken, or turkey)

½ tsp kosher salt

¼ tsp black pepper

1 tsp ground cumin

1 tsp sweet paprika

½ cup chopped fresh parsley

½ cup pine nuts (optional)

¾ cup tahini sauce (for recipe, see p. 34)

Method

1. Preheat oven to 400°F. Spray a large rectangular oven-to-table baking dish with nonstick cooking spray.

2. **Eggplant:** Arrange eggplants, cut side up, in a single layer in baking dish. Score exposed flesh of eggplants with a sharp knife, making a crisscross design about 1-inch deep. Brush with olive oil and sprinkle with salt and pepper.

3. Bake, uncovered, for 25-30 minutes, until tender.

4. **Meat:** Meanwhile, heat oil in a large nonstick wok or skillet over medium heat. Add onion and garlic; sauté for 5 minutes, until golden.

5. Add ground beef, salt, pepper, cumin, paprika, parsley, and pine nuts, if using. Cook for 8-10 minutes, stirring often, until beef is browned and cooked through.

6. **Assembly:** Spoon about ½ cup meat mixture onto each eggplant half.

7. Cover loosely with foil and bake for 25-30 minutes.

8. Drizzle with tahini sauce; serve hot.

Norene's Notes

- Variation: Use 6-8 large zucchini, halved lengthwise, instead of eggplant. Scoop out the seeds, if you like, to make room for the meat filling.

When the weather turns chilly, there's nothing like a steaming bowl of hot chili! Although most people consider it to be a main dish, it's fun to serve chili as a hearty starter with tortilla chips on the side.

Chunky Chili

meat | gluten-free | freezes well | yields 6 servings

Ingredients

2 Tbsp grapeseed or vegetable oil

1 lb/500 g lean ground beef (or ground veal, chicken, or turkey)

2 onions, diced

2 red bell peppers, diced

2 stalks celery, thinly sliced

6 cloves garlic, minced (about 1 Tbsp)

1 Tbsp unsweetened cocoa powder

2 Tbsp chili powder

1 tsp ground cumin

½ tsp cayenne (or to taste)

1 can (28 oz/796 ml) diced tomatoes, with their liquid

2 cans (19 oz/540 ml each) red kidney beans, drained and rinsed

2 tsp kosher salt

½ tsp black pepper

tortilla chips, optional

Method

1. Heat oil in a large pot or wok on medium-high heat. Add ground beef; cook for 6-8 minutes or until browned, stirring often to break up meat.

2. Stir in onions, peppers, celery, and garlic; cook for 5 minutes longer, until vegetables have softened, stirring often.

3. Add cocoa, chili powder, cumin, cayenne, tomatoes with their liquid, beans, salt, and pepper. Bring to a boil.

4. Reduce heat; simmer, covered, for about 1 hour, stirring occasionally. Adjust seasonings to taste.

5. Spoon into individual ramekins or a large bowl; serve with tortilla chips if desired.

Norene's Notes

- Variation: Serve over rice or quinoa.
- Slow Cooker Method: Follow steps 1 and 2 above. Transfer sautéed meat and vegetables to a slow cooker insert coated with nonstick cooking spray. Add remaining ingredients and stir well. Cover; cook on low setting for 6-8 hours.

This is a new spin on an old classic. Sometimes comfort food is all you really need!

Quick Skillet Dinner

meat | passover option | gluten-free | freezes well | yields 6-8 servings

Ingredients

1 Tbsp vegetable or olive oil

2 lb/1 kg lean ground beef (or ground veal, chicken, or turkey)

2 onions, chopped

2 cloves garlic, minced (about 1 tsp)

1 red bell pepper, chopped

2 stalks celery, chopped

1 medium zucchini, chopped (do not peel)

1 can (28 oz/796 ml) tomatoes, with their liquid

2 tsp kosher salt

½ tsp black pepper

1 tsp dried basil

1¼ cups rice or quinoa, rinsed and drained (use quinoa for Passover)

Method

1. Heat oil in a large pot, Dutch oven, or wok over medium-high heat. Add ground beef; cook for 5-7 minutes, or until browned, stirring often.

2. Add onions, garlic, pepper, celery, zucchini, tomatoes with their liquid, salt, pepper, and basil. Stir well to combine. Heat until simmering. Stir in rice or quinoa.

3. Reduce heat; simmer, covered, for about 30 minutes, stirring occasionally.

Norene's Notes

- The food processor chops the vegetables in moments.
- If you use brown rice, increase the cooking time to 40-45 minutes.
- Variation: Add 1 can (19 oz/540 ml) kidney beans or chickpeas, rinsed and drained. Canned baked beans also work well.

Dairy

For nutritional information on this section, see page 325

These yummy bites are packed with healthy and delightful goodness. Kid-friendly, but not kid-specific, these savory mouthfuls work as snacks, appetizers, or even cute, bite-sized sides. I serve three with a salad for a light lunch.

Cheesy Quinoa Bites

dairy | passover | gluten-free | freezes well | yields about 3 dozen mini muffins

Ingredients

3 cups water

1½ cups quinoa, rinsed and drained

3 eggs, lightly beaten

1 cup shredded carrots

½ cup diced red onion

3 scallions, thinly sliced

2 cloves garlic, minced (about 1 tsp)

¼ cup chopped fresh parsley

1 cup shredded mozzarella or Cheddar cheese

2 Tbsp grated Parmesan cheese

1 tsp kosher salt

¼ tsp black pepper

Method

1. Bring water to a boil in a medium saucepan over high heat. Add quinoa; reduce heat. Simmer, covered, for 15 minutes, or until tender. Remove from heat and let stand 5 minutes. Fluff with a fork. Transfer to a large serving bowl; let cool.

2. Preheat oven to 350°F. Coat interior of mini muffin pans with nonstick cooking spray.

3. Add eggs, carrots, red onion, scallions, garlic, parsley, cheeses, salt, and pepper to cooled quinoa. Mix well.

4. Fill prepared muffin pans to the top with quinoa mixture and flatten slightly.

5. Bake, uncovered, for 20-25 minutes or until edges are golden-brown.

6. Cool slightly and remove from muffin pans. Serve warm or at room temperature.

Norene's Notes

- In a hurry? Chop the carrots, onions, scallions, garlic, and parsley in the food processor.
- Some brands of quinoa do not require rinsing. Otherwise, rinse under running water for 1 minute to remove the bitter coating (saponin).

Who doesn't like bread smothered in melted cheese? Spectacularly simple, this loaf is gooey and delicious — just what a cheese bread should be. Serve with a hearty vegetable soup or a simple salad.

Gourmet Garlicky Cheesy Bread

dairy | gluten-free option | freezes well | yields 8 servings

Ingredients

1 baguette or round loaf, unsliced (gluten-free or regular)

2 cups shredded mozzarella or Cheddar cheese

¼ cup butter, melted

3 scallions, thinly sliced

3 cloves garlic, minced (about 1½ tsp)

½ tsp chili flakes (or to taste)

Method

1. Preheat oven to 350°F. Line a baking sheet with a piece of foil large enough to enclose the entire loaf.

2. Using a serrated knife, cut loaf into a tic-tac-toe design: First, without cutting all the way through the bottom crust, cut loaf lengthwise, spacing cuts 1 inch apart. Then, still without cutting through the bottom crust, cut loaf crosswise, also spacing cuts 1 inch apart. Place loaf onto foil.

3. In a small bowl, combine cheese, butter, scallions, garlic, and chili flakes; mix well.

4. Spoon most of cheese mixture between cuts in the loaf. Sprinkle loaf with remaining mixture. Wrap loaf loosely with foil.

5. Bake 15 minutes. Unwrap and bake an additional 10 minutes, or until cheese is golden and bubbling. Serve hot.

Norene's Notes

- Variation: Make individual servings by using rolls instead of a large loaf. Reduce baking time slightly.

- You can shred and grate your own cheese and freeze any extra for 2-3 months. Squeeze out excess air from the package to prevent ice crystals from forming. No need to thaw cheese before using it. If it is clumped together, hit it against the counter a few times to break it up.

Only four ingredients, yet these smashed, cheese-drizzled taters are mouthfuls of comfort and joy. My kids are in food heaven every time I make a batch. Serve as cute appetizer bites at parties, or as a scrumptious side dish with fish.

Cheesy Smashed Roasted Potatoes

dairy | passover | gluten-free | do not freeze | yields 6 servings

Ingredients

24 mini potatoes (1½ lb/750 g)

2 Tbsp olive oil

kosher salt

freshly ground black pepper

2 cups shredded mozzarella or Cheddar cheese

Method

1. Preheat oven to 400°F. Line a rimmed baking sheet with parchment paper.

2. Arrange potatoes in a single layer on prepared baking sheet. Bake, uncovered, for 45 minutes, or until a skewer can be inserted easily into the largest potatoes.

3. Place a large piece of parchment paper over potatoes. Place a second baking pan or cookie sheet on the parchment; press down gently, flattening each potato to about half of its original thickness. Remove pan and parchment paper.

4. Drizzle smashed potatoes with olive oil; sprinkle with salt and pepper. Top with cheese. (See Norene's Notes, below.)

5. Bake, uncovered, an additional 10 minutes or until cheese is golden and bubbling.

Norene's Notes

- Variation: Make Mini Pizza Taters by drizzling each smashed potato with tomato sauce and sprinkling with cheese. Top with minced scallions and red bell peppers.
- To shred cheese in a food processor, freeze cheese first for 15 minutes. Use medium pressure on pusher when grating. No food processor? Use a box grater.
- Four ounces (120 g) cheese yields 1 cup shredded.

When I was a kid, this cheesy-good dish was a staple in our house. Since my little ones love it so much, I've maintained that tradition. The cauliflower is tender-crisp and slightly crunchy, thanks to panko crumbs and melted cheese.

Double Cheese Cauliflower Gratin

dairy | passover option | gluten-free option | do not freeze | yields 4-6 servings

Ingredients

1 large cauliflower, trimmed, cut into florets

kosher salt

freshly ground black pepper

1 cup panko crumbs (gluten-free or regular)

2 cups shredded Cheddar or mozzarella cheese (8 oz/250 g)

½ cup grated Parmesan cheese

Method

1. Preheat oven to 375°F. Coat a 10-inch round ceramic or glass quiche dish with nonstick cooking spray.

2. Place cauliflower into a vegetable steamer. Steam for 12-15 minutes, or until tender-crisp. Alternatively, place cauliflower in a large saucepan with enough water to cover. Bring to a boil, reduce heat, and simmer, covered, for 15 minutes. Drain well; cool slightly.

3. Arrange florets in a single layer in prepared dish. Sprinkle with salt, pepper, panko crumbs, and cheeses.

4. Bake, uncovered, for 25-30 minutes, until golden-brown and bubbling.

Norene's Notes

- For a pretty presentation, use a combination of cauliflower and broccoli florets.
- Passover Option; Replace panko crumbs with matzo meal (gluten-free or regular), or simply omit the crumbs.
- A whole cauliflower takes 10-12 minutes, covered, to microwave on high power.
- Substitute a 20-oz bag of frozen cauliflower florets for the whole cauliflower. No need to defrost before using.

Halfway between a spanakopita and a quiche, this spinach-feta tart is a longtime brunch favorite. It's perfect for a buffet table, but also makes a great side dish when you are serving a plated meal.

Crustless Spinach & Feta Cheese Tart

dairy | passover | gluten-free | do not freeze | yields 6-8 servings

Ingredients

1 lb/500 g baby spinach
(about 10 cups)
(see Norene's Notes, below)

2 cloves garlic

1 large onion, quartered

1 cup crumbled feta cheese

4 eggs

¼ tsp black pepper

Method

1. Preheat oven to 350°F. Lightly coat bottom and sides of a 10-inch glass or ceramic quiche dish with nonstick cooking spray.

2. Wash and drain spinach. Roll the spinach in a clean, dry towel; squeeze out water.

3. In a food processor fitted with the steel blade, process garlic and onion until minced. Add spinach, feta, eggs, and pepper. Process just until combined, 12-15 seconds (see Norene's Notes, below).

4. Pour mixture into prepared pan; spread evenly.

5. Bake, uncovered, for 40-45 minutes, or until top is set and edges are golden-brown. Serve hot or at room temperature.

Norene's Notes

• If using frozen spinach in this recipe, use 1½-2 packages (10-ounce/300 g each). Just thaw spinach and squeeze dry.

• No food processor? In step 3, finely chop garlic, onion, and spinach with a chef's knife; combine with feta, eggs, and pepper in a bowl. Mix well.

Gourmet made easy! This scrumptious salad, with its fresh, flavorful ingredients, is a staple in my kitchen. No matter how many times we eat this, we never get bored with the soft mozzarella, juicy tomatoes, and aromatic basil.

Caprese Penne Salad

dairy | gluten-free option | do not freeze | yields 6-8 servings

Ingredients

1 pkg (16 oz/454 g) penne pasta (gluten-free or regular)

1 pint cherry tomatoes, halved

8 oz/250 g mozzarella cheese, cut into bite-sized chunks (about 2 cups)

½ cup chopped fresh basil

additional basil, for garnish

Dressing

½ cup extra virgin olive oil

½ cup balsamic vinegar

2 cloves garlic, minced (about 1 tsp)

1 tsp kosher salt

¼ tsp black pepper

¼ tsp chili flakes (or to taste)

Method

1. Cook pasta al dente in salted water according to package directions. Drain well.

2. Transfer pasta to a serving bowl; let cool. Add tomatoes, mozzarella, and basil.

3. **Dressing:** Combine ingredients for salad dressing in a glass jar; seal tightly and shake well.

4. Toss salad with dressing. Adjust seasonings to taste. Garnish with additional basil leaves. Serve chilled.

Norene's Notes

- Quick Tip: Instead of cutting a block of mozzarella into chunks, use individual cheese sticks and slice crosswise into bite-sized pieces.
- Variation: Make Bocconcini Kabobs by marinating cut-up mozzarella cheese and whole cherry tomatoes in dressing for 20 minutes. Alternate them on small wooden skewers, adding small whole basil leaves in between. Serve chilled as an appetizer. Easy cheesy!

From garnish to side dish to centerpiece, a rustic vine of roasted tomatoes adds bold colors and flavors to any meal. After a few minutes in the oven, these morsels emerge brighter and sweeter in taste than their uncooked cousins.

Roasted Balsamic Tomatoes & Feta Cheese

dairy | passover | gluten-free | do not freeze | yields 4-6 servings

Ingredients

2 lb/1 kg small tomatoes on the vine

2 Tbsp extra virgin olive oil

1 tsp kosher salt

½ tsp black pepper

1 cup coarsely crumbled feta cheese

2 Tbsp balsamic vinegar

Method

1. Preheat oven to 400°F. Line a rimmed baking sheet with parchment paper.

2. Arrange tomatoes on the vine in a single layer on prepared baking sheet. Drizzle with olive oil; season with salt and pepper.

3. Bake, uncovered, for 12-15 minutes, or until they start to collapse.

4. Transfer carefully to a large serving platter. Sprinkle with feta cheese; drizzle with balsamic vinegar or balsamic glaze (see Norene's Notes, below).

Norene's Notes

- Never store tomatoes in the refrigerator, unless they are super-ripe. Keep them on a kitchen counter out of direct sunlight until ready to use.
- To make balsamic glaze, pour ¼ cup balsamic vinegar into a small saucepan. Bring to a boil; reduce heat and simmer until thick and syrupy and it has reduced by half.

With just a few simple ingredients, the sweetness of the berries really shines through. Serve this for weekday breakfasts or midday snacks. It has just enough protein to keep me going and just enough sweetness to keep me smiling.

Fresh Berry Toast

dairy | gluten-free option | do not freeze | yields 2-4 servings

Ingredients

2 cups strawberries
(thaw if using frozen)

1 Tbsp honey or agave

4 slices bread
(gluten-free or regular)

1 cup ricotta, goat cheese,
or Yogurt Cheese,
at room temperature
(see Norene's Notes, below)

Method

1. In a small bowl, lightly mash berries until chunky. Add honey; stir well.

2. Toast bread to desired doneness.

3. Spread with cheese and top with berry spread.

Norene's Notes

- To make Yogurt Cheese, line a large strainer with a paper coffee filter or cheesecloth; place over a bowl. Spoon in 2 cups plain yogurt. Cover, refrigerate (with the bowl), and let drain. In 3-4 hours you will have Greek yogurt and in 24 hours you will have firm-textured Yogurt Cheese (similar in texture to cream cheese). Don't discard the whey that drips out. It can be used as a buttermilk replacement in baked goods!

I really love the way noodles twirl around a fork. If I'm having company, I often serve this dish on small plates as a first course. It's fabulous with fish, especially Fresh Salmon Patties (p. 18).

Lemon Garlic Spaghetti

dairy | gluten-free option | do not freeze | yields 4 servings

Ingredients

1 pkg (12 oz/340 g) spaghetti (gluten-free or regular)

⅓ cup extra virgin olive oil

4 cloves garlic, minced (about 2 tsp)

juice of **1** lemon (about 3 Tbsp)

1 tsp kosher salt, or to taste

freshly ground black pepper

½ cup chopped fresh parsley or basil

½ cup grated Parmesan cheese

½ cup panko crumbs (gluten-free or regular)

Method

1. Cook pasta al dente according to package directions. Drain well.

2. Heat oil in the same pot over medium heat (no need to wash the pot). Add garlic; sauté until fragrant, 1-2 minutes.

3. Return pasta to pot. Add lemon juice, salt, pepper, and parsley. Toss to combine. Stir in Parmesan cheese and panko crumbs.

4. Serve immediately.

Norene's Notes

- Variations: Instead of spaghetti, substitute different pasta shapes (gluten-free or regular). If you like it spicy, shake in some chili flakes.

- Spaghetti squash noodles are an excellent gluten-free option. See page 56 for instructions on how to prepare them.

Penne · Spaghetti · Ravioli · Linguine · Penne · Spaghetti · Ravioli · Linguine ·

Make a perfect, thin crust pizza — with a surprising twist! Swap the wheat-based crust for a crispy cauliflower alternative. Topped with spinach and mozzarella, this gluten-free pizza is just as cheesy and delicious as the real thing.

Cauliflower-Crusted Pizza

dairy | passover | gluten-free | do not freeze | yields 4-6 servings

Ingredients

Crust

1 medium cauliflower, cut into florets

1 egg, lightly beaten

½ cup shredded mozzarella cheese

¼ cup grated Parmesan cheese

1 tsp kosher salt

freshly ground black pepper

½ tsp dried oregano

½ tsp dried basil

Topping

¾ cup tomato or pizza sauce

2 cups shredded mozzarella cheese

fresh basil leaves

Method

1. Place cauliflower florets into a food processor fitted with the steel blade. Pulse for 30-40 seconds, until fine. Measure 2½ cups.

2. Microwave cauliflower in a microwaveable bowl, covered, on high for 3-4 minutes. Alternatively, steam for 10-12 minutes.

3. Transfer to a clean tea towel and cool slightly. Wrap tightly; squeeze out as much water as possible.

4. Preheat to 425°F. Line a pizza pan or baking sheet with parchment paper.

5. Place dried cauliflower into a bowl; add egg, cheeses, salt, pepper, oregano, and basil. Mix well.

6. Spread mixture evenly onto prepared pan; pat down firmly, forming a 10-12-inch circle.

7. Bake 20-25 minutes, or until golden and set.

8. Remove pan from oven. Spread tomato sauce evenly over crust. Sprinkle with cheese; top with basil leaves. Bake an additional 8-10 minutes or until cheese is melted, golden, and bubbly.

Norene's Notes

• For a crisp crust, preheat the baking sheet or pizza pan.

This is for the Norene Gilletz fans. These muffins and their variations have become staples in many families around the world. Thanks for sharing your Grandma's treasured recipe, Aviva Bursten Cohen of Winnipeg.

Grandma Marion's Cheese Muffins

dairy | passover option | gluten-free option | freezes well | yields about 15 muffins

Ingredients

2 cups/500 ml small curd cottage cheese

1 stick (½ cup) melted butter

3 eggs

4-6 Tbsp sugar (to taste)

2 tsp baking powder

pinch salt

1 tsp cinnamon

1½ cups flour (or gluten-free flour with xanthan gum)

Method

1. Preheat oven to 350°F. Coat muffin compartments with nonstick cooking spray or line with paper liners.

2. In a large bowl, mix together cottage cheese, butter, eggs, sugar, baking powder, salt, and cinnamon.

3. Gradually add flour, mixing until well combined.

4. Scoop batter into prepared muffin pans, filling them three-quarters full.

5. Bake about 35 minutes, or until golden.

Norene's Notes

- Variation: Bake miniature muffins at 375°F for 20-25 minutes.
- Passover Option: Substitute 1 cup + 2 tsp potato starch for flour.
- Lighter version: Use ¼ cup oil or melted butter. Lower fat cottage cheese works perfectly here. Sugar substitutes also work well in this recipe.
- Add 1 cup blueberries or any berry of your choice. Chocolate chips also work well in this recipe.

Grain
Side Dishes

For nutritional information on this section, see pages 325–326

The bright flavors and crunchy textures of this colorful, autumn-inspired dish bring just the right amount of sweetness to a meal.

Apple-Cranberry Couscous

pareve | gluten-free option | do not freeze | yields 4-6 servings

Ingredients

1½ cups Israeli couscous (about one 8.8 oz pkg) (see Norene's Notes, below)

½ green apple, julienned (do not peel)

½ red apple, julienned (do not peel)

1 Tbsp lemon juice (preferably fresh)

¾ cup dried cranberries

½ cup candied almonds or pecans (optional) (p. 280)

Dressing

¼ cup extra virgin olive oil

¼ cup apple cider vinegar

2 Tbsp honey or pure maple syrup

1 tsp kosher salt

freshly ground black pepper

Method

1. Cook couscous according to package directions. Fluff with a fork; let cool.

2. In a serving bowl, toss apples with lemon juice. Add couscous and cranberries.

3. Dressing: Combine ingredients for dressing in a glass jar; seal tightly, and shake well.

4. Add dressing to couscous mixture and mix well. Top with almonds, if using. Serve chilled or at room temperature.

Norene's Notes

- To make this dish gluten-free, use brown rice couscous, quinoa, kasha, or a rice blend; cook according to package directions.
- Israeli couscous is actually toasted pasta and originated in Israel. It is also known as pearl couscous or maftoul.

This simple pilaf, infused with delicious Middle Eastern flavors, is great as a side dish or a meal-in-a-bowl. Tangy lemon zest and bright green parsley bring these protein-packed legumes to life.

Lemon-Infused Lentil Rice

pareve | gluten-free | freezes well | yields 8 servings

Ingredients

3 cups water

1 cup dry brown lentils, rinsed and drained

2 cups lightly salted water

1 cup basmati rice, rinsed and drained

2 Tbsp olive oil

2 medium onions, halved and thinly sliced

1 can (19 oz/540 g) chickpeas, drained and rinsed

1 cup chopped fresh flat-leaf parsley or cilantro

Dressing

1 Tbsp fresh lemon zest

juice of **2** lemons (about ½ cup)

2 Tbsp extra virgin olive oil

1 Tbsp kosher salt

freshly ground black pepper

1 tsp ground cumin (optional)

additional parsley or cilantro, for garnish

Method

1. In a medium saucepan, bring 3 cups water to a boil over high heat. Add lentils; reduce heat. Simmer, covered, for 30-45 minutes, until lentils are tender but not mushy. (See Norene's Notes, below.)

2. In a second saucepan, bring 2 cups lightly salted water to a boil over high heat. Stir in rice; reduce heat. Simmer, covered, for 20 minutes. Remove from heat and let stand, covered, for 10 minutes. Fluff rice with a fork.

3. In a large wok, heat oil over medium heat. Sauté onions for 10-12 minutes, or until nicely browned.

4. Add lentils, rice, chickpeas, and parsley. Mix well; remove from heat.

5. **Dressing:** In a medium bowl, combine ingredients for dressing. Pour over rice mixture; stir to combine.

6. Transfer to a serving bowl; garnish with parsley. Serve hot or at room temperature.

Norene's Notes

- Cooking time for lentils will vary, depending on age and dryness of lentils. If your water is very hard, cook them in bottled water or they will be slow to soften. Also, don't add salt to the cooking water or the lentils won't soften.

- Short on time? Substitute 1 can (19 oz/540 ml) lentils, rinsed and drained. Rinsing them well under cold water will cut the amount of sodium in half.

Curry is such an easy way to make ordinary rice extraordinary! With its rich aroma and bright colors, this simple rice dish is the perfect starting place if you're a curry beginner.

Curried Basmati Pilaf

pareve | gluten-free | freezes well | yields 4 servings

Ingredients

2 cups water or vegetable broth

1 cup basmati rice (white or brown), rinsed and drained

2 Tbsp olive oil

1 large onion, diced

4 cloves garlic, minced (about 2 tsp)

1 tsp curry powder

1 tsp turmeric

½ tsp ground cinnamon

¾ cup dried cranberries or raisins

kosher salt

freshly ground black pepper

sliced scallions, for garnish

toasted slivered almonds, for garnish

Method

1. Bring water to a boil in a medium saucepan over high heat. Add rice; reduce heat and simmer, covered, until tender. White basmati rice will take 20 minutes; brown basmati will take about 35 minutes. Remove from heat and let stand, covered, for 10 minutes. Fluff rice with a fork.

2. Heat oil in a nonstick wok or large skillet over medium heat. Add onion and garlic; sauté for 5-7 minutes, or until golden.

3. Stir in cooked rice, curry powder, turmeric, cinnamon, and dried cranberries. Season with salt and pepper.

4. Transfer to a serving bowl; sprinkle with scallions and almonds. Serve hot or at room temperature.

Norene's Notes

- Curry powder is a blend of spices that usually includes coriander, turmeric, cumin, fenugreek, and red pepper. Turmeric, the main ingredient in curry powder, gives it a wonderful flavor and a vivid yellow color.

- Turmeric is an excellent anti-inflammatory and antioxidant, with many health benefits. It has been found to help prevent or alleviate Alzheimer's disease, arthritis, and many kinds of cancer.

Dark, unique, and unexpected, this fabulous dish will wow the guests at your next dinner party. The bright, tropical colors of the fruit contrast beautifully with the black rice, making a stunning presentation.

Black Rice
with mango, pomegranate & avocado

pareve | gluten-free | do not freeze | yields 6-8 servings

Ingredients

3 cups lightly salted water

1½ cups black rice, rinsed and drained

2 ripe mangoes, peeled, pitted, and diced (about 2 cups)

¾ cup pomegranate seeds

4 scallions, thinly sliced

¼ cup chopped fresh basil

1 ripe Hass avocado

Dressing

⅓ cup extra virgin olive oil

⅓ cup pomegranate or orange juice

2 Tbsp honey or agave

2 tsp Dijon mustard

kosher salt

freshly ground black pepper

Method

1. Bring water to a boil in a medium saucepan over high heat. Add rice; reduce heat. Cover and simmer for 35-40 minutes. The rice should be tender but slightly chewy. Remove from heat, let stand, covered, for 10-15 minutes. Transfer to a large serving bowl; let cool.

2. Add mangoes, pomegranate seeds, scallions, and basil to the serving bowl.

3. **Dressing:** Combine ingredients for dressing in a glass jar; seal tightly and shake well.

4. Shortly before serving, peel, pit, and dice avocado. Add avocado and dressing to rice mixture; toss gently to combine. Serve at room temperature.

Norene's Notes

- In China, black rice was called "forbidden rice," as it was considered the finest grain and served only to the royal family.

- How to seed a pomegranate: Score around the middle of the pomegranate, but do not cut through. Twist to separate pomegranate into two halves. Invert one half in your palm over a bowl, seeds facing down. With a wooden spoon, firmly tap the skin several times to release the seeds into the bowl. Pick out and discard the white pith. Repeat with second pomegranate half. Seeds will keep fresh for 2-3 days in the fridge in a covered container.

- Instead of mangoes, substitute 2 cans (11 oz/312 g each) mandarin oranges, well-drained.

This dish is elegant, eye-catching and, most importantly, simple to make. When topped with crunchy candied almonds, this delicious side goes from ordinary to extraordinary.

Wild Rice
with roasted peppers & candied almonds

pareve | gluten-free | freezes well | yields 8 servings

Ingredients

4 cups water

1½ cups wild rice, rinsed and drained

1 tsp kosher salt

2 red bell peppers, halved and sliced

1 large onion, halved and sliced

2 Tbsp olive oil

kosher salt

freshly ground black pepper

4 cloves garlic, minced (about 2 tsp)

zest and juice of **1** lemon

1 cup candied whole or sliced almonds (p. 280)

Method

1. Bring water to a boil in a medium saucepan over high heat. Add rice and salt; cover and simmer for about 45 minutes, or until the grains split and burst. Remove from heat; let stand, covered, for 10 minutes. Transfer to a large bowl or heatproof baking dish.

2. Meanwhile, preheat oven to 400°F. Line a rimmed baking sheet with parchment paper.

3. Spread peppers and onion slices in a single layer on prepared baking sheet. Drizzle with oil; sprinkle with salt, pepper, and garlic; toss to combine. Roast, uncovered, for 25-30 minutes, or until edges of vegetables are slightly charred.

4. Add roasted vegetables to wild rice. Add lemon zest and juice; toss together. Adjust seasonings to taste.

5. Top with candied almonds at serving time. Serve hot or at room temperature.

Norene's Notes

- Wild rice is not actually rice, but rather a long-grain grass. It has a nutty flavor, is gluten-free, and is high in protein, fiber, and B vitamins. Did you know that wild rice has double the protein of brown rice?

- Black rice, also known as forbidden rice, works well in this recipe. (Follow cooking instructions on p. 210.)

This quintessential medley is bright in color, fresh in flavor, and tastes terrific. Hearts of palm add a silky yet firm texture to this simple side.

Quinoa
with hearts of palm, cherry tomatoes & avocado

pareve | passover | gluten-free | do not freeze | yields 8 servings

Ingredients

3 cups lightly salted water

1½ cups quinoa, rinsed and drained

½ cup diced red onion

1 can (14 oz/400 g) sliced hearts of palm, well-drained

2 cups cherry tomatoes, halved

1½ cups chopped fresh spinach

1 ripe avocado

Dressing

⅓ cup extra virgin olive oil

⅓ cup lemon juice (preferably fresh)

2 Tbsp honey

2 cloves garlic, minced (about 1 tsp)

1 tsp kosher salt

freshly ground black pepper

Method

1. Bring water to a boil in a medium saucepan over high heat. Add quinoa; reduce heat. Simmer, covered, for 15 minutes or until tender. Remove from heat; let stand, covered, for 10 minutes. Fluff quinoa with a fork. Transfer to a large serving bowl; let cool.

2. Add onion, hearts of palm, tomatoes, and spinach to quinoa.

3. Dressing: Combine ingredients for dressing in a glass jar; seal tightly and shake well.

4. Shortly before serving, peel, pit, and dice avocado. Add avocado and dressing to quinoa mixture; toss gently to combine. Adjust seasonings to taste. Serve chilled or at room temperature.

Norene's Notes

- Nutritional tip: Quinoa provides life-sustaining nutrients, including all 8 essential amino acids, so it is a complete protein. It is gluten-free, making it an excellent alternative for those who are allergic to wheat.

- Use quinoa as a replacement for rice, couscous, bulgur, or wheat berries in salads and side dishes.

The pickled onions take just moments to make, so don't be intimidated. The combination of juicy nectarines and pickled onions adds a sweet and tangy taste to this dish. Our recipe testers loved it!

Quinoa
with nectarines & pickled onions

pareve | passover | gluten-free | do not freeze | yields 8 servings

Ingredients

Pickled Onions

¾ cup water

¾ cup apple cider vinegar

2 Tbsp honey

2 tsp kosher salt

1 medium red onion, thinly sliced

Quinoa

3 cups lightly salted water

1½ cups quinoa, rinsed and drained

2-3 large ripe nectarines, diced (do not peel)

2 cups baby spinach, roughly chopped

3 Tbsp extra virgin olive oil

1 tsp kosher salt

¼ tsp black pepper

Method

1. **Pickled Onions:** Combine water, vinegar, honey, and salt in a medium saucepan; bring to a boil. Stir in sliced onion. Remove from heat; let cool.

2. **Quinoa:** Meanwhile, bring water to a boil in another medium saucepan over high heat. Add quinoa and reduce heat. Simmer, covered, for 15 minutes, or until tender. Remove from heat; let stand, covered, for 10 minutes. Fluff with a fork.

3. Drain onions, reserving ⅓ cup pickling liquid. Place onions into a large serving bowl. Add quinoa, nectarines, and spinach.

4. Combine reserved pickling liquid with oil, salt, and pepper in a glass jar. Seal tightly and shake well.

5. Shortly before serving, add dressing to quinoa mixture and toss to combine. Serve chilled or at room temperature.

Norene's Notes

- Variation: You can sub the quinoa with any other grain. Try it with a rice blend (white and brown basmati, wild and red rice) or kasha (but not for Passover)!
- Variation: Peaches, apricots, mangoes, or mandarin oranges can be substituted for the nectarines.
- The pickled onions are scrumptious, so why not make a double batch and add them to your favorite salad! Stored with their liquid in a closed container, pickled onions will stay fresh for about 2 weeks.

The sweet dried fruit and crisp fresh cabbage make an unexpected but blissful match in this colorful dish. Great as a side dish or a lighter main, this healthy salad is ideal for lunches, picnics, or potlucks.

Quinoa
with dried fruit & red cabbage

pareve | gluten-free | do not freeze | yields 8 servings

Ingredients

3 cups lightly salted water

1½ cups quinoa (red or white), rinsed and drained

2 cups shredded red cabbage

1 cup dried apricots and/or mangoes, thinly sliced

¾ cup dried cranberries

4 scallions, thinly sliced

Dressing

6 Tbsp extra virgin olive oil

3 Tbsp soy sauce or tamari

3 Tbsp rice vinegar

2 Tbsp honey or agave

Method

1. Bring water to a boil in a medium saucepan over high heat. Add quinoa; reduce heat. Simmer, covered, for 15 minutes, or until tender. Remove from heat; let stand, covered, 10 minutes. Fluff quinoa with a fork. Transfer to a large serving bowl; let cool.

2. Add cabbage, apricots, cranberries, and scallions to cooled quinoa.

3. Dressing: Combine ingredients for dressing in a glass jar; seal tightly and shake well.

4. Toss quinoa mixture with dressing shortly before serving. Serve chilled or at room temperature.

Norene's Notes

- Quinoa is one of the new superfoods. It is thought of as a grain, but technically it is a seed.
- Red and black quinoa call also be used in any recipe calling for quinoa.

With five different roasted veggies, this colorful dish is great for a crowd. It's a cross between a salad and a side dish that's vegan-friendly, protein-rich, and gluten-free.

Quinoa
with roasted veggies

pareve | passover | gluten-free | do not freeze | yields 10 servings

Ingredients

Roasted Vegetables

1 medium red onion, diced

1 red bell pepper, diced

1 zucchini, diced (do not peel)

1 small sweet potato, peeled and diced

4 cloves garlic, minced (about 2 tsp)

2 Tbsp olive oil

kosher salt

freshly ground black pepper

Quinoa

3 cups lightly salted water

1½ cups quinoa, rinsed and drained

Dressing

⅓ cup extra virgin olive oil

⅓ cup balsamic vinegar

2-3 Tbsp honey

1½ tsp kosher salt

¼ tsp black pepper

Method

1. Preheat oven to 400°F. Line a rimmed baking sheet with parchment paper.

2. In a large bowl, combine onion, bell pepper, zucchini, sweet potato, and garlic. Drizzle with oil, sprinkle with salt and pepper, and toss to combine.

3. Spread in a single layer on prepared baking sheet. Roast, uncovered, for 35-45 minutes, until golden.

4. Meanwhile, bring water to a boil in a medium saucepan over high heat. Add quinoa and reduce heat. Simmer, covered, for 15 minutes or until tender. Remove from heat and let stand for 10 minutes, covered. Fluff quinoa with a fork.

5. **Dressing:** Combine ingredients for dressing in a glass jar; seal tightly and shake well.

6. In a serving bowl, combine cooked quinoa with roasted veggies and dressing. Mix well. Serve hot or at room temperature.

Norene's Notes

• Variation: Instead of quinoa, use a rice blend, couscous (gluten-free or regular), or kasha (but not for Passover).

When you want to serve a side dish with an Asian flair but are rushed for time, try this vegetable-noodle combo. For a less spicy version, omit the chili flakes and sriracha.

Rice Noodles
with crunchy veggies

pareve | gluten-free | do not freeze | yields 8 servings

Ingredients

1 pkg (10 oz/300 g)
rice noodles
(see Norene's Notes, below)

2 cups shredded red cabbage

1 cup shredded carrots

4 scallions, thinly sliced

¾ cup toasted pumpkin seeds
or sunflower seeds

3 Tbsp black or white
sesame seeds

Dressing

¼ cup extra virgin olive oil

¼ cup rice vinegar

3 Tbsp soy sauce or tamari

2 tsp toasted sesame oil

¼ tsp chili flakes (or to taste)

1 tsp sriracha sauce (optional)

Method

1. Cook rice noodles according to package directions. They only take about 2 minutes to cook. Drain well. (If not using immediately, cover noodles with cold water and set aside. Drain well before using.)

2. Place noodles into a large serving bowl. Add cabbage, carrots, and scallions.

3. Dressing: Combine ingredients for dressing in a glass jar; seal tightly and shake well.

4. Add dressing to noodle mixture; toss to combine.

5. Add pumpkin seeds and sesame seeds before serving. Toss to combine. Serve at room temperature.

Norene's Notes

- Thin rice noodles are also called vermicelli: thicker ones are called sticks or ribbons. Rice noodles have a soft texture and can be used in hot or cold dishes.
- Soba noodles have a nutty flavor and will work well in this recipe. They are made from buckwheat flour, but some brands contain wheat flour, so check labels carefully if you are on a gluten-free diet.

Fresh, simple, packed with power-foods — what an easy way to serve up healthy ingredients. This favorite lunch option gives you a ton of energy without feeling stuffed. Wheat berries take an hour or more to cook, so prepare them in advance.

Wheat Berries
with kale & mango

pareve | gluten-free option | do not freeze | yields 6 servings

Ingredients

1 cup wheat berries, rinsed and drained (see Norene's Notes, below)

3 cups lightly salted water

3 cups kale, trimmed, chopped into bite-sized pieces

½ cup diced red onion

1 mango, peeled, pitted, and diced

½ cup dried cranberries

Dressing

¼ cup extra virgin olive oil

¼ cup rice vinegar

2 Tbsp lemon juice (preferably fresh)

2 cloves garlic, minced (about 1 tsp)

kosher salt

freshly ground black pepper

Method

1. Combine wheat berries with lightly salted water in a saucepan; bring to a boil. Reduce heat to low; cover and simmer for 1-1½ hours, or until tender. Drain excess liquid, if any. Transfer to a large bowl; let cool. Can be made one day in advance.

2. Add kale, onion, mango, and cranberries.

3. **Dressing:** Combine ingredients for dressing in a glass jar; seal tightly and shake well.

4. About an hour before serving, toss wheat berry mixture with dressing. Serve chilled or at room temperature.

Norene's Notes

- Gluten-Free Option: Replace wheat berries with brown rice, gluten-free pasta, quinoa, brown rice couscous, or kasha (buckwheat groats). Cook according to package directions.
- Variation: For a non-gluten-free option, replace wheat berries with millet, couscous, or pasta.
- Kale is a nutritional powerhouse. It's healthful, low in calories, high in fiber, packed with nutrients, high in iron ... who can ask for anything more! This salad also works well with baby kale, spinach, or romaine lettuce.

Vegetable Side Dishes

For nutritional information on this section, see pages 326–327

This dish has spectacular flavors. The roasted garlic becomes smooth, creamy, and sweet, accentuating the earthy flavors of the asparagus.

Roasted Asparagus & Garlic

pareve | passover | gluten-free | do not freeze | yield 6-8 servings

Ingredients

2 heads garlic
(24-30 cloves), peeled
(see Norene's Notes, below)

3 Tbsp olive oil, divided

kosher salt

freshly ground black pepper

2 bunches asparagus
(about 2 lb/1 kg)

3 scallions, thinly sliced

juice of ½ lemon

Method

1. Preheat oven to 400°F.

2. Place garlic cloves onto a large piece of foil. Drizzle with 1 tablespoon olive oil; sprinkle lightly with salt and pepper. Wrap well.

3. Roast for 30 minutes, or until tender.

4. Meanwhile, line a rimmed baking sheet with parchment paper. Bend asparagus stalks; snap off the tough ends where they naturally break. Discard ends.

5. Spread asparagus in a single layer on baking sheet. Sprinkle with scallions and drizzle with remaining olive oil. Season lightly with salt and pepper.

6. Roast, uncovered, for 10-12 minutes or until asparagus is tender-crisp.

7. In a serving dish, combine asparagus with roasted garlic cloves; drizzle with lemon juice. Serve hot or at room temperature.

Norene's Notes

- To peel garlic easily, place a head of garlic on a cutting board and cover with a dishtowel. Firmly hit the towel-covered garlic with the bottom of a heavy skillet. Remove the towel, separate the cloves, and pick out the papery skins. Repeat several times if necessary, discarding any remaining skins.

- An average head of garlic contains 12-15 cloves. Peeled garlic cloves are available in many supermarkets. Roast a big batch of garlic cloves and refrigerate them up to 10 days. Add them to salads, salad dressings, or shmear on bread or crackers (regular or gluten-free).

Crunchy asparagus spears and three different kinds of sautéed mushrooms transform a simple stir-fry into a simply elegant dish. It's ideal for an Asian-inspired menu or a rustic-style meal. For maximum flavor, make it when fresh asparagus is in season.

Asparagus & Mushroom Stir-Fry

pareve | gluten-free | do not freeze | yields 8-10 servings

Ingredients

2 bunches asparagus (about 2 lb/1kg)

2-3 Tbsp toasted sesame oil

2 cups sliced button or cremini mushrooms

2 cups sliced shiitake mushrooms

2 cups sliced portobello mushrooms

4 cloves garlic, minced (about 2 tsp)

kosher salt

freshly ground black pepper

2 Tbsp black or white sesame seeds

Method

1. Bend asparagus stalks; snap off the tough ends where they break off naturally. Discard ends. Cut stalks diagonally into 1-inch pieces.

2. Heat oil in a nonstick wok or large skillet over medium-high heat.

3. Add asparagus and mushrooms; stir-fry for 6-8 minutes, until tender-crisp. Add garlic; cook 1 minute longer. Season with salt and pepper.

4. Transfer to a serving bowl; sprinkle with sesame seeds. Serve hot or at room temperature.

Norene's Notes

• One bunch of asparagus weighs about 1 lb/500 g and will serve 4. There are 16 to 20 spears per pound.

• Look for asparagus spears that are all the same thickness so they will cook evenly. The thinner the spear, the more quickly it cooks.

• Asparagus wrapped in a damp paper towel and stored in the refrigerator will keep fresh for up to two weeks.

• Garlic acts as a natural antibiotic. To optimize its benefits, let it sit for 10-15 minutes after mincing it.

Everybody loves green beans. When you add in Asian-inspired ingredients such as ginger, soy, and sesame, this will quickly become one of your go-to recipes. It's the kind of dish that people will ask you to make again and again.

Crunchy Gingered Green Beans

pareve | gluten-free | do not freeze | yields 6-8 servings

Ingredients

2 Tbsp grapeseed oil

2 lb/1 kg thin green beans (haricots verts), ends trimmed

2 cloves garlic, minced (about 1 tsp)

2 tsp chopped fresh ginger

2 Tbsp soy sauce or tamari

2 Tbsp toasted sesame seeds

Method

1. Heat oil in a nonstick wok over medium-high heat. Add green beans and stir-fry for 3-5 minutes, or until tender-crisp.

2. Add garlic, ginger, and soy sauce; stir-fry for 2 minutes.

3. Transfer to a serving dish; sprinkle with sesame seeds. Serve hot or at room temperature.

Norene's Notes

• Green beans are low in calories and a rich source of dietary fiber; they are packed with vitamins and nutrients.

• Variation: In step 2, add 2 tsp toasted sesame oil for a different twist.

• If overcooked, the green beans will lose their bright green color and crisp texture.

This is a terrific way to enjoy bok choy. The crunchy panko topping is always a hit, and the simple cooking technique used for the bok choy makes it a snap to prepare.

Panko-Topped Bok Choy & Edamame

pareve | gluten-free option | do not freeze | yields 6 servings

Ingredients

3 Tbsp toasted sesame oil, divided

¾ cup panko crumbs (gluten-free or regular)

8 baby bok choy, halved lengthwise, ends trimmed

1 pkg (12 oz/340 g) frozen shelled edamame beans (do not thaw)

2 cloves garlic, minced (about 1 tsp)

½ tsp kosher salt

¼ tsp black pepper

Method

1. Topping: In a small saucepan, heat 1 tablespoon oil over low heat. Add panko crumbs and toast for 3-5 minutes, until golden brown. (Can be done in advance; store in airtight container in fridge or freezer.)

2. Heat remaining oil in a nonstick wok or large skillet on medium-high heat. Add bok choy, edamame, and garlic. Sauté for 3-5 minutes, or until bok choy is tender-crisp. Stir in salt and pepper.

3. Transfer bok choy mixture to a serving dish and sprinkle with panko crumbs. Serve hot or at room temperature.

Norene's Notes

- Baby bok choy has a sweeter, more delicate flavor than regular bok choy; however, baby bok choy is usually more expensive. To prevent overcooking if using regular bok choy, sauté the stems first, then add the leaves.

- Bok choy contains certain antioxidant plant chemicals that help protect against breast, colon, and prostate cancers. It also helps to reduce blood cholesterol levels, so go for green!

My family loves these glazed green slices for their sweet taste and crunchy texture. A departure from traditional cabbage recipes, this one retains that comfort-food feel for which cabbage is famous, yet looks elegant on a serving platter.

Maple-Dijon Cabbage Rounds

pareve | gluten-free | do not freeze | yields 6-8 servings

Ingredients

1 head green cabbage (about 2 lb/1 kg)

⅓ cup olive oil

⅓ cup pure maple syrup

1 Tbsp Dijon mustard

2 cloves garlic, minced (about 1 tsp)

kosher salt

freshly ground black pepper

Method

1. Preheat oven to 425°F. Line a large rimmed baking sheet with parchment paper.

2. Peel off and discard outer leaves from cabbage. Core the cabbage; then slice it from top to bottom into 1-inch thick rounds. If cabbage rounds are very large, cut them in half. Place in a single layer onto prepared baking sheet.

3. **Glaze:** In a small bowl, combine oil, maple syrup, mustard, and garlic; stir well to combine.

4. Using a pastry brush, evenly coat both sides of cabbage slices with glaze. Sprinkle with salt and pepper.

5. Bake, uncovered, for 40-45 minutes, until lightly browned and glazed.

6. Using a wide spatula, carefully transfer cabbage to a large serving platter. Serve hot or at room temperature.

Norene's Notes

• The end pieces will fall apart slightly, so save them as a nosh for the cook!
• Leftovers? Add them to your favorite vegetable soup.

The best thing about a roasted cauliflower is the absolute ease with which it's made. Simply spiced, this cauliflower pairs with everything. Looks great, tastes amazing.

Spiced Cauliflower

pareve | passover | gluten-free | do not freeze | yields 6 servings

Ingredients

1 large cauliflower

2 Tbsp brown sugar

1½ tsp kosher salt

½ tsp black pepper

1 tsp garlic powder

1 tsp onion powder

2 tsp sweet paprika

⅛ tsp chili flakes (or to taste)

2 Tbsp olive oil

Method

1. Preheat oven to 400°F. Line a rimmed baking sheet with parchment paper.

2. Cut cauliflower into 2-inch florets. Transfer to prepared baking sheet.

3. In a small bowl, combine brown sugar, salt, pepper, garlic powder, onion powder, paprika, and chili flakes. Mix well.

4. Sprinkle spices over cauliflower florets; drizzle with olive oil. Rub all over to coat evenly.

5. Bake, uncovered, for 35-40 minutes, or until cauliflower is golden brown and tender.

6. Carefully transfer cauliflower to a serving platter. Serve hot or at room temperature.

Norene's Notes

• Frozen cauliflower florets work well in this recipe; no need to defrost before using.

• This tasty spice rub also goes beautifully with chunks of sweet potato and acorn squash.

These savory roasted onions pair perfectly with fish, chicken, turkey, beef — even as a pizza topping! With three types of onions in a lemony maple-Dijon dressing and roasted until golden, this dish is ideal when my menu needs a little oomph. Yum!

Herb-Roasted Dijon Onions

pareve | gluten-free | do not freeze | yields 4-6 servings

Ingredients

3 Tbsp olive oil

3 Tbsp lemon juice (preferably fresh)

2 Tbsp Dijon mustard

3 Tbsp pure maple syrup or honey

4 cloves garlic, minced (about 2 tsp)

kosher salt

freshly ground black pepper

2 Tbsp chopped fresh parsley

2 medium red onions, cut into wedges

3 medium yellow onions, cut into wedges

3-4 shallots, cut into wedges

Method

1. Preheat oven to 400°F. Line a large rimmed baking sheet with parchment paper.

2. In a large bowl, whisk together oil, lemon juice, mustard, maple syrup, garlic, salt, pepper, and parsley. Add onions and shallots; toss carefully to coat them.

3. Spread onions and shallots in a single layer on prepared baking sheet. Roast, uncovered, for 35-40 minutes, or until glazed and golden.

Norene's Notes

- If you store onions in a cool dry place with good air circulation, they will keep for months.

- The compounds in onions can bring you to tears! Refrigerate or freeze onions for 15 minutes. When peeling, trim off the roots at the last moment. You can also peel onions under cold water to help minimize tears.

- Eyeglasses or onion goggles will help act as a barrier to onion fumes. Some people hold a burnt match between their teeth for that purpose.

Everyone loves latkes! Festive enough for Chanukah, but casual enough for year-round meals, parsnip latkes are a wonderful way to enjoy a different spin on this traditional Jewish delicacy.

Parsnip Potato Latkes

dairy | passover option | gluten-free option | freezes well | yields 12-15 large latkes

Ingredients

1 lb/500 g parsnips, peeled (2-4, depending on size)

1 large potato, peeled (preferably Idaho/russet)

1 medium onion

2 eggs

¼ cup flour (or gluten-free flour with xanthan gum)

1 tsp baking powder

1 tsp kosher salt

¼ tsp black pepper

2 Tbsp chopped fresh dill

grapeseed or vegetable oil, for frying

Sour Cream Dill Topping

1½ cups sour cream or Greek yogurt

1 Tbsp lemon juice (preferably fresh)

3 Tbsp chopped fresh dill

freshly ground black pepper

additional dill for garnish

Method

1. Preheat oven to 250°F. Line a rimmed baking sheet with parchment paper.

2. In a food processor fitted with the shredding disk, shred parsnips, potato, and onion, using medium pressure. Transfer vegetables to a large colander and press firmly to drain excess liquid.

3. Place veggies into a large bowl. Add eggs, flour, baking powder, salt, pepper, and dill. Mix well.

4. In a large skillet, heat oil over medium-high heat. Working in batches, drop large spoonfuls of batter into hot oil to form pancakes, flattening them slightly with the back of the spoon. Do not crowd the skillet. Fry for 3-4 minutes per side or until golden.

5. Drain well on paper towels. Transfer to prepared baking sheet and place into oven to keep warm.

6. **Topping:** Stir together sour cream, lemon juice, dill, and pepper. Place into a serving bowl; garnish with additional dill. Serve with latkes.

Norene's Notes

- Latkes freeze well. To reheat, place frozen latkes onto a large baking sheet. Bake, uncovered, at 400°F for 10-15 minutes, or until hot and crispy. If the latkes weren't frozen, reheating time will be slightly less.

- Passover Option: Use 3 Tbsp potato starch instead of flour and use Passover baking powder. You can omit the baking powder, but the latkes won't be quite as light.

This beautiful dish is packed with healthy goodness. The mini potatoes come out golden on the outside and smooth and creamy on the inside, almost melting in your mouth. The tiny roasted tomatoes provide a contrast to the mix with their bright, bold flavor.

Roasted Baby Potato & Tomato Medley

pareve | passover | gluten-free | do not freeze | yields 6 servings

Ingredients

2 lb/1 kg fingerling or baby potatoes, scrubbed and halved (about 2 dozen)

1 cup red grape tomatoes

1 cup yellow grape tomatoes

4 cloves garlic, minced (about 2 tsp)

2 tsp chopped fresh thyme

2 Tbsp olive oil

kosher salt

freshly ground black pepper

Method

1. Preheat oven to 425°F. Line a rimmed baking sheet with parchment paper.

2. In a large bowl, combine potatoes, tomatoes, garlic, and thyme. Drizzle with olive oil; sprinkle generously with salt and pepper. Stir gently to combine.

3. Spread vegetables in a single layer on prepared baking sheet. Roast, uncovered, for 45-50 minutes, or until potatoes are golden. They should be tender when pierced with a sharp knife. Serve hot.

Norene's Notes

- Fingerling potatoes remain relatively small even when full grown, so they're a great choice for roasting.

- Potatoes are very high in potassium, a good source of iron and copper, and so satisfying. They are also believed to help fight depression.

- If your potatoes are tinged with green, cut off and discard any green parts. The green layer under the skin is called solanin and is poisonous.

- Tomatoes are high in lycopene, which gives tomatoes their bright red color. When tomatoes are cooked, more of the lycopene becomes available — and we like that!

This simple potatonik (kugel) comes from my great-grandmother, Florence Fisher, lovingly called Great Bub. This dish is the star of every holiday table. With its crunchy, golden outer shell and gooey, creamy, yummy center, this is "the best of the best."

Great Bub's Overnight Potatonik

pareve | passover | gluten-free | do not freeze | yields 10-12 servings

Ingredients

5 lb Idaho (russet) potatoes, peeled (about 12-15 medium potatoes)

2 large onions, halved

3 eggs

1½ Tbsp kosher salt (or to taste)

3 Tbsp olive oil

Method

1. Preheat oven to 350°F. Grease the bottom and partway up the sides of a large deep ovenproof casserole, or spray with nonstick spray. (I use a Le Creuset 5-quart pot.)

2. In a food processor fitted with the shredding disk, shred potatoes and onions, using medium pressure. You will have to do this in batches.

3. Transfer potatoes and onions to a large bowl. Add eggs and salt; mix well to combine.

4. Spoon mixture into prepared casserole and spread evenly. Drizzle oil evenly over top.

5. Bake, covered, for 8-10 hours or overnight. About 1 hour before serving, uncover casserole and continue to bake until top of potatonik has a golden-brown crust.

Norene's Notes

- If you grate the potatoes and onions alternately, the potatoes will stay white.

- Russet potatoes are the best choice for this recipe. They are high in starch and have lower water content, so you don't need to add potato starch or flour.

- What's the Difference: Dry, mealy potatoes have a high starch content and are perfect for baked or mashed potatoes. Waxy potatoes have a lower starch content and are best for boiling, scalloped potatoes, or potato salad. If you don't know which type of potato you have, put it in a brine of 2 Tbsp salt plus 1½ cups cold water. Mealy potatoes will sink; waxy ones will float.

This simple, unassuming scallop is both sweet and savory. Using sweet potatoes instead of white makes it a healthier option. As a final bonus, the elegant upright presentation gives the dish some textural interest that's worthy of any holiday feast.

Sweet Potato Scallop

pareve | passover | gluten-free | do not freeze | yields 8 servings

Ingredients

¼ **cup** olive oil

¼ **cup** honey

1 tsp ground cinnamon

2 tsp chopped rosemary

6 medium sweet potatoes, thinly sliced (do not peel)

kosher salt

freshly ground black pepper

Method

1. Preheat oven to 400°F. Coat a large oven-to-table baking dish with nonstick cooking spray.

2. In a large bowl, combine oil, honey, cinnamon, and rosemary. Add sweet potatoes; sprinkle lightly with salt and pepper. Stir to coat on all sides.

3. Arrange sweet potato slices in prepared baking dish by standing them upright in tight rows. You should have parallel lines of sweet potato slices (skin showing) along the length of the dish. Drizzle with any remaining oil mixture.

4. Bake, covered, for 45 minutes.

5. Bake, uncovered, an additional 20-30 minutes, until golden and glazed.

Norene's Notes

- Variation: Sprinkle sweet potato slices generously with salt and pepper. Add 3 Tbsp olive oil, 2 Tbsp honey, and ¼ cup chopped fresh basil or dill. Stir well. Arrange sweet potato slices in baking dish as directed in step 3. Bake, covered, for 45 minutes. Uncover; bake 20-30 minutes longer.

- Quick Tip: The sweet potatoes can be sliced with a food processor, using medium pressure.

This brightly colored side dish combines a unique pairing of roasted roots with vibrant, juicy fruits. A few basil leaves and a splash of orange juice add a refreshing finish that goes perfectly with that savory roasted flavor.

Rainbow Roasted Roots
with oranges & pomegranates

pareve | passover | gluten-free | do not freeze | yields 8 servings

Ingredients

2 bunches red or rainbow beets, scrubbed and trimmed (about 6-8 beets)

3 medium sweet potatoes, peeled, cut into 1-inch chunks

3 parsnips, peeled, trimmed, cut into 1-inch chunks

2 Tbsp olive oil

kosher salt

freshly ground black pepper

2 seedless oranges, peeled and cut into 1-inch chunks

⅓ cup pomegranate seeds

½ cup orange juice

2 Tbsp olive oil

2 Tbsp honey

¼ cup chopped fresh basil

Method

1. Preheat oven to 400°F. Cut a large piece of heavy-duty foil; place onto a rimmed baking sheet.

2. Coat foil with nonstick cooking spray. Place beets onto center of foil; wrap tightly, pinching edges together. Roast for about 1 hour, until tender.

3. Spread sweet potatoes and parsnips in a single layer on a parchment-lined baking sheet. Drizzle with oil; sprinkle with salt and pepper. Roast, uncovered, for 40-45 minutes, or until tender. (You can roast them at the same time as the beets.)

4. Carefully open foil packet and let beets stand until cool enough to handle. Use paper towels to rub off skins. Discard the skins. Cut beets into 1-inch chunks and place into a large serving bowl. Season with salt and pepper.

5. Add sweet potatoes, parsnips, oranges, and pomegranate seeds.

6. Add orange juice, oil, honey, and basil. Toss together gently. Serve at room temperature.

Norene's Notes

- Variation: Instead of sweet potatoes, use squash, carrots, or baby pumpkin, cut into chunks. Instead of parsnips, use 1 lb/500 g baby potatoes, halved. Measurements don't need to be too exact. You just want a variety of different-colored vegetables.

- Variation: No pomegranate seeds? Add ½ cup dried cranberries.

- Variation: Substitute 1 can (398 ml/14 oz) pineapple chunks, drained, for oranges.

This unique combo of squash and roasted pears brings something new to the table. A perfect partner to roast chicken or brisket, this simple veggie side dish is always well received.

Roasted Squash
with red onion & pears

pareve | passover | gluten-free | do not freeze | yields 8 servings

Ingredients

2 large delicata squash
(about 1 lb/500 g each)

1 large red onion,
halved and sliced

4 firm ripe pears (e.g., Bosc),
cored, cut into wedges
(do not peel)

2 Tbsp olive oil

3 Tbsp brown sugar
or honey

1 tsp sweet paprika

kosher salt

freshly ground black pepper

Method

1. Preheat oven to 425°F. Line a rimmed baking sheet with parchment paper.

2. Cut squash in half lengthwise and scoop out the seeds. Cut squash crosswise into ¼-inch slices to form half moons.

3. In a large bowl, combine squash with onion and pears. Drizzle with olive oil; sprinkle with brown sugar, paprika, salt, and pepper. Stir gently.

4. Spread mixture in a single layer on prepared baking sheet.

5. Roast, uncovered, for about 30-35 minutes, just until tender, turning squash, onion, and pears once or twice during cooking.

6. Transfer to a serving platter. Serve hot or at room temperature.

Norene's Notes

• Delicata is a winter squash with dark green stripes on a yellow or cream-colored background. Its flesh is orange/yellow, so it's often called sweet potato squash. It's a good source of fiber and potassium.

• If you can't find delicata squash, substitute acorn squash.

Sneak in some extra veggie-fueled protein with these scrumptious mini kugels. Spinach is full of energy-boosting nutrients, so creative ways to serve the leafy green are always a good idea.

Zucchini-Spinach Kugels

pareve | gluten-free option | freezes well | yields about 22 kugels

Ingredients

4 eggs

1 cup vegetable oil
(or ½ cup oil and ½ cup unsweetened applesauce)

¾ cup sugar

2 tsp pure vanilla extract

2 cups flour (or gluten-free flour with xanthan gum)

1 tsp baking soda

2 tsp baking powder

pinch kosher salt

1 tsp ground cinnamon

3-4 medium zucchini
(do not peel)
(about 4 cups grated)

2 cups packed fresh spinach leaves

Method

1. Preheat oven to 350°F. Coat compartments of muffin pans with nonstick cooking spray (see Norene's Notes, below).

2. In a large bowl, combine eggs, oil, sugar, and vanilla. Mix well.

3. Stir in flour, baking soda, baking powder, salt, and cinnamon.

4. Using a food processor fitted with the grating blade, grate zucchini, using medium pressure. Measure 4 cups and add to batter.

5. Process spinach on the steel blade for 10-12 seconds, until minced. (No need to wash the bowl first.) Add to batter and mix well.

6. Spoon batter into prepared muffin pans, filling each compartment about three-quarters full.

7. Bake for 35-40 minutes or until golden. Serve hot or at room temperature.

Norene's Notes

- If there are any unfilled muffin compartments, fill them halfway with water to prevent muffin pan from burning.
- One medium zucchini yields about 1 cup when grated.
- Variation: Replace zucchini with grated butternut squash or carrots.

Cookies, Squares, & Treats

For nutritional information on this section, see pages 327–328

With the crispy crackle and the nutty crunch of almonds, these delicious cookies are sweet and sensational. Using only three simple ingredients, you can have a whole batch ready in less than 25 minutes — no mess, no stress.

1-2-3 Almond Cookies

parve | passover | gluten-free | freezes well | yields about 4 dozen cookies

Ingredients

2 egg whites

⅔ cup sugar

4 cups slivered or sliced almonds

Method

1. Preheat oven to 300°F. Line two baking sheets with parchment paper.

2. In a medium bowl, use a fork to stir together egg whites and sugar. Gently stir in almonds.

3. Drop mixture from a teaspoon onto prepared baking sheets, forming small mounds.

4. Bake for 20 minutes or until crisp and golden. Let cool on baking sheet. Store at room temperature in airtight container.

Norene's Notes

• Variation: Top each cookie with a chocolate chip before baking.

• Leftover yolks? Use 2 yolks to replace each egg in baking, or use them in omelets.

Chocolate chip cookies were a tried-and-true treat in my mom's house. This is our ultimate version of her original recipe. These are incredible!

Ultimate Chocolate Chip Cookies

pareve | dairy option | gluten-free option | freezes well | yields 15-18 large cookies

Ingredients

2 cups flour
(or gluten-free flour with xanthan gum)

1 tsp baking soda

1 tsp baking powder

¾ tsp sea salt

1 cup vegetable oil

¾ cup granulated sugar

¾ cup brown sugar, lightly packed

2 eggs

2 tsp pure vanilla extract

2½ cups chocolate chips

additional sea salt, for sprinkling (optional)

Method

1. In a medium bowl, combine flour with baking soda, baking powder, and salt.

2. In the bowl of an electric mixer fitted with the paddle attachment, beat together oil and sugars on medium-high speed until light, about 5 minutes. Beat in eggs one at a time, mixing well after each addition. Blend in vanilla.

3. Reduce speed to low; add flour mixture. Mix just until combined, 10-15 seconds. Fold in chocolate chips.

4. Press plastic wrap against the surface of dough; refrigerate for 24-36 hours.

5. Preheat oven to 350°F. Line 2 large baking sheets with parchment paper.

6. Using a large cookie scoop, drop mounds of dough the size of golf balls onto prepared baking sheets, leaving 2 inches between each mound. Sprinkle lightly with sea salt, if using.

7. Bake for 12-14 minutes, until golden brown but still soft. Let cool on baking sheet. Store at room temperature in an airtight container.

Norene's Notes

- Dairy Variation: Replace chocolate chips with 1½ cups chocolate chunks or white chocolate and 1 cup toffee bits.
- If baking two pans at once, place oven racks to divide oven evenly into thirds; switch pans halfway through baking, from front to back and from top rack to bottom rack.

These home-style cookies are one of my long-time favorites. The sweetness of the dried apricots and white chocolate is balanced by the oats. Perfectly unique and always a hit!

White Chocolate Chip & Dried Apricot Cookies

pareve | gluten-free option | freezes well | yields 12-15 large cookies

Ingredients

½ **cup** vegetable oil

½ **cup** brown sugar, lightly packed

¼ **cup** granulated sugar

1 egg

1 tsp pure vanilla extract

¾ **cup** flour (or gluten-free flour with xanthan gum)

1½ **cups** rolled oats (regular or gluten-free)

½ **tsp** baking soda

pinch kosher salt

1 cup dried apricots, cut into chunks (see Norene's Notes, below)

1 cup white chocolate chips

Method

1. Preheat oven to 350°F. Line two baking sheets with parchment paper.

2. In the bowl of an electric mixer fitted with the paddle attachment, beat oil with sugars, egg, and vanilla on medium speed until well blended.

3. Add flour, oats, baking soda, and salt. Mix on low speed for 30-60 seconds, just until combined.

4. Add apricots and white chocolate chips. Mix on lowest speed just until combined.

5. Using a large cookie scoop, form dough into golf ball size mounds; place 2 inches apart on prepared baking sheets. Press gently to flatten each ball. (See Norene's Notes, below.)

6. Bake for 12-15 minutes, until golden. Let cool on baking sheet. Store at room temperature in an airtight container.

Norene's Notes

- An easy way to cut dried apricots is to use kitchen scissors.
- Pantastic! In step 5, cover balls of cookie dough with a sheet of parchment paper, then top with another baking sheet. Press gently to flatten. Uncover and bake as directed.

These cookies are a staple in my house. I always have a batch stashed in my freezer — they taste fabulous frozen! The cranberry and chocolate combo is just amazing — tart and sweet!

Chocolate Chunk Cranberry Cookies

pareve | gluten-free option | freezes well | yields about 18-20 large cookies

Ingredients

¾ cup vegetable oil

1 cup brown sugar, lightly packed

½ cup sugar

2 eggs

1 tsp pure vanilla extract

1¾ cups flour (or gluten-free flour with xanthan gum)

1 tsp baking soda

pinch kosher salt

1½ cups chocolate chunks (or chocolate chips)

1 cup dried cranberries

Method

1. In the bowl of an electric mixer fitted with the paddle attachment, beat oil, sugars, eggs, and vanilla on medium speed until light.

2. Add flour, baking soda, and salt. Mix on low speed, just until blended, 30-60 seconds.

3. Add chocolate chunks and cranberries; mix just until combined.

4. Cover and refrigerate for 45 minutes, until chilled. (The dough will keep in the refrigerator for up to 2 days.)

5. Preheat oven to 350°F. Line two baking sheets with parchment paper.

6. Using a large cookie scoop, drop mounds of dough the size of golf balls 2 inches apart onto prepared baking sheets.

7. Bake for 12-14 minutes, until golden. Let cool on baking sheet. Store at room temperature in an airtight container.

Norene's Notes

- Brown or white? Brown sugar has a higher moisture content than white sugar. Using more brown sugar produces softer, chewier cookies. Using more white sugar produces cookies that are flatter and crispier.

- Chill out: If you chill your cookie dough before baking, the cookies will spread more slowly during baking. That's because the heat sets the cookie while it's still thick, producing a denser, chewier cookie.

- For chewier cookies, cool cookie sheets between each batch. If your cookie sheets are hot when you add the cookie batter, the cookies will spread more.

These fabulous flourless cookies are little bites of heaven. Studded with white chocolate chips, they deliver rich, chocolaty goodness. They're a snap to make, and when they come out of the oven, they're chewy and delicious.

Flourless Fudgy-Wudgy Cookies

pareve | passover | gluten-free | freezes well | yields about 30 cookies

Ingredients

2⅓ cups confectioner's sugar

1 cup unsweetened cocoa powder

pinch kosher salt

3 egg whites

2 tsp pure vanilla extract

1 cup white chocolate chips (see Norene's Notes, below)

Method

1. Preheat oven to 350°F. Line two baking sheets with parchment paper.

2. In a large bowl, combine sugar, cocoa, and salt.

3. Add egg whites and vanilla. Mix well, forming a sticky dough. Stir in white chocolate chips.

4. Using a small cookie scoop, drop dough by rounded spoonfuls onto prepared baking sheets, leaving 2 inches between each cookie.

5. Bake for about 10 minutes, or until set. Let cool on the baking sheet. Remove from pan with a flexible spatula. Store in an airtight container in the refrigerator or freezer (they thaw quickly).

Norene's Notes

- You can get dairy-free white chocolate chips, even for Passover. Chopped pecans or almonds are a delicious addition or substitution.

- You can substitute liquid egg whites in this recipe. Use 2 tablespoons for each egg white.

These bite-sized treats are fairly low in calories and are the perfect way to satisfy your sweet tooth. Crispy rice cereal adds a crunch and is available gluten-free.

Chocolate Chip Meringue Clouds

pareve | passover option | gluten-free option | freezes well | yields 2 dozen

Ingredients

2 egg whites,
at room temperature

¾ cup sugar

1 tsp pure vanilla extract

1½ cups crispy rice cereal
(regular or gluten-free)

1 cup mini or regular
chocolate chips

Method

1. Preheat oven to 325°F. Line 2 baking sheets with parchment paper.

2. In the bowl of an electric mixer fitted with the whisk attachment, beat egg whites on medium speed until frothy.

3. Increase mixer speed to medium-high; gradually add sugar, beating in 1 tablespoon at a time, until whites are stiff and glossy. The meringue should look like marshmallow. Beat in vanilla.

4. Using a rubber spatula, fold in rice cereal and chocolate chips.

5. Drop batter by rounded tablespoons onto prepared baking sheets, leaving 2 inches between cookies.

6. Bake for 12-15 minutes, or until dry to the touch. Let cool on baking sheet. Store at room temperature in an airtight container.

Norene's Notes

- Egg White Wisdom: Eggs separate best when they are cold and whip best when they are at room temperature. Be sure that no yolks get into the whites or they won't whip properly. Use a glass or metal bowl rather than plastic. The bowl and beaters must be clean and grease-free. When egg whites are beaten to the proper stiffness, you can turn the bowl upside down without the whites falling out.

- Passover Option: Use Passover cereal (e.g. Crispy-O's) or slivered almonds. Use Passover vanilla.

Although I love my own biscotti, I'm not sure they can compete with my mother-in-law Bonny Silver's incredible version. Crushed cornflakes add a wonderful crunchy texture. She always brings a huge batch and always leaves empty-handed.

Cranberry-Cornflake Biscotti

pareve | gluten-free option | freezes well | yields about 30 slices

Ingredients

2 eggs

1 cup vegetable oil

1 cup sugar

1 tsp pure vanilla extract

2 cups flour
(or gluten-free flour with xanthan gum)

2 tsp baking powder

¼ tsp kosher salt

1 cup coarsely crushed cornflakes
(regular or gluten-free)

1 cup dried cranberries

1½ tsp ground cinnamon mixed with **¼ cup** sugar, for sprinkling

Method

1. Preheat oven to 350°F. Line a large rimmed baking sheet with parchment paper.

2. In a large mixing bowl, whisk together eggs, oil, sugar, and vanilla until well blended. Stir in flour, baking powder, and salt. Gently stir in cornflakes and cranberries.

3. Transfer half the dough to baking sheet and shape into a long, narrow log (about 1½ inches wide). Repeat with second half of dough, leaving about 3 inches between logs, as they spread during baking. Smooth tops and sides.

4. Bake for 25-30 minutes, or until light brown. Remove from oven; let cool for 10-15 minutes.

5. Reduce oven temperature to 300°F. Using a serrated knife, cut logs into slices about ¾-inch thick. Turn slices cut side up; sprinkle with cinnamon-sugar.

6. Bake for 20 minutes, until golden.

Norene's Notes

• You can coarsely crush cornflakes with your hands before measuring.

• Variation: Instead of cranberries, substitute dried cherries or blueberries. Chocolate chips or slivered almonds are also wonderful add-ins.

• Make an extra batch of cinnamon-sugar and store it in a spice jar. Shake and bake!

Whenever I'm hosting a dinner party, I always like to include some kind of crunchy, gourmet cookie on my dessert table. Not too sweet, with just the right amount of chocolate, these biscotti are a delicious after-dinner hit.

Pistachio Biscotti

pareve | gluten-free option | freezes well | yields 5 dozen slices

Ingredients

3 eggs

¾ cup vegetable oil

1 cup sugar

1 tsp pure vanilla extract

1 tsp instant coffee granules

2½ cups flour
(or gluten-free flour with xanthan gum)

2 tsp baking powder

¼ tsp kosher salt

1 tsp ground cinnamon

1 cup finely chopped pistachios

1 cup chocolate chips
or white chocolate chips

Chocolate Coating

2 cups chocolate chips
or white chocolate chips, melted

½ cup finely ground pistachios

Method

1. Preheat oven to 350°F. Line one or two large rimmed baking sheets with parchment paper.

2. In a large mixing bowl, whisk together eggs, oil, sugar, vanilla, and coffee granules until well blended.

3. Add flour, baking powder, salt, and cinnamon; mix to make a soft dough. Stir in pistachios and chocolate chips.

4. Divide dough into thirds. Place one-third onto baking sheet; shape into long, narrow logs. Repeat with remaining dough, leaving about 3 inches between logs, as they spread during baking. Smooth out tops and sides.

5. Bake for 25-30 minutes or until golden. Remove from oven and let cool for 5-10 minutes.

6. Reduce oven temperature to 275°F. Using a serrated knife, cut logs into slices about ¾-inch thick. Turn slices cut side up. Bake an additional 30 minutes, until dry and crisp. Let cool.

7. **Chocolate Coating:** Spoon melted chocolate on one side of each slice; spread evenly with the back of the spoon. Sprinkle with pistachios. Refrigerate 15 minutes, until chocolate has set.

8. Store in an airtight container in the refrigerator or freezer.

Norene's Notes

• Variation: Use toasted almonds instead of pistachios. For a nut-free option, omit nuts; increase chocolate chips in dough to 2 cups.

• Variation: Dip each cookie halfway into melted chocolate instead of spooning it over the top.

These chewy bars are a household favorite! Enjoy them with tea or coffee, or grab one on the go. I like to switch them up by using different jams. If you have a nut allergy, omit almonds.

Chewy Raspberry-Oatmeal Bars

pareve | gluten-free option | freezes well | yields about 3 dozen

Ingredients

1 cup vegetable oil

1 cup brown sugar, lightly packed

1 egg

1 tsp pure vanilla extract

2 cups flour
(or gluten-free flour with xanthan gum or almond meal flour)

2 cups rolled oats
(gluten-free or regular)

2 tsp baking powder

½ cup sliced almonds (optional)

1 jar (12 oz/340 g) raspberry jam

Method

1. Preheat oven to 350°F. Line a 9 x 13-inch baking pan with parchment paper or spray with nonstick spray.

2. In the bowl of an electric mixer fitted with the paddle attachment, beat together oil, sugar, egg, and vanilla for 1-2 minutes, until light. (You can also mix this in a large bowl, using a wooden spoon, or in a food processor.)

3. Add flour, oats, baking powder, and almonds, if using. Mix together to form a crumbly mixture.

4. Reserve 1 cup of crumb mixture for topping. Press remaining mixture evenly into bottom of pan to form a base.

5. Spoon jam evenly over base, spreading it carefully so that base is not disturbed. Sprinkle with reserved crumbs.

6. Bake 30-35 minutes, or until golden.

7. Let cool for 15-20 minutes. Cut into long, narrow strips.

Norene's Notes

- Variations: Substitute apricot or strawberry jam for raspberry. For chocolate lovers, sprinkle 1 cup chocolate chips over base in step 5.

- Doubly Good! To double the recipe, use a 12 x 18-inch rimmed baking sheet lined with parchment paper. Baking time is about the same.

Sweet with a touch of salty, gooey with a surprising crunchy topping, these fudgy, pretzel-topped brownies have all your favorites covered. A huge hit at bake sales, parties, and potlucks, these brownies look as good as they taste.

Fudgy Pretzel Brownies

pareve | dairy option | gluten-free option | freezes well | yields about 2 dozen

Ingredients

1 cup flour
(or gluten-free flour with xanthan gum)

¾ cup unsweetened cocoa powder

pinch kosher salt

½ tsp baking powder

3 eggs

1 cup vegetable oil

1 cup brown sugar, lightly packed

¾ cup granulated sugar

2 tsp pure vanilla extract

about 24 whole pretzels, salted or unsalted (gluten-free or regular)

Glaze

½ cup semisweet or white chocolate chips

1 tsp vegetable oil

Method

1. Preheat oven to 325°F. Spray a 9 x 13-inch baking pan with nonstick cooking spray.

2. In a medium bowl, whisk together flour, cocoa, salt, and baking powder.

3. In a large bowl, whisk together eggs, oil, sugars, and vanilla until well blended. Add flour mixture and stir just until combined.

4. Spread batter evenly in prepared pan. Arrange a layer of whole pretzels over batter.

5. Bake 28-30 minutes, or until a toothpick comes out almost clean. Cool slightly.

6. **Glaze:** In a small saucepan over low heat, melt chocolate chips with oil. Drizzle glaze in a zigzag design over pretzel-topped brownies. Cool completely before cutting into squares.

Norene's Notes

- Variation: For Black & White Brownies, add 1 cup white chocolate chips to brownie batter. Bake as directed.

- Variation: For Caramel Pretzel Brownies (Dairy), prepare and bake brownie batter as directed above, but do not top with whole pretzels and do not glaze. For caramel topping, combine 1 bag (14 oz/396 g) unwrapped caramels, ¼ cup butter, and 1 Tbsp milk in a saucepan. Melt over low heat, stirring often. Immediately pour caramel mixture over warm baked brownies. Let cool. Sprinkle ½ cup chocolate chips and 1 cup crushed pretzels over caramel.

These chocolate barks are beautiful and taste amazing — and they freeze well, too!

Coconut Rocky Road Bark

pareve | passover | gluten-free | yields 8 servings

Ingredients

1 bar (14 oz/400 g) semisweet chocolate, broken into chunks

1½ cups miniature marshmallows

1½ cups whole almonds

1½ cups shredded unsweetened coconut

Method

1. Line a baking sheet with parchment paper.

2. Pour about 1 inch of water into a saucepan. Bring to a boil; reduce heat to a simmer.

3. Place chocolate into a large, dry, heatproof bowl wider than the saucepan. Place bowl over simmering water. Melt chocolate, stirring often. Cool slightly.

4. Stir in marshmallows, almonds, and coconut. Pour mixture onto prepared pan; spread evenly.

5. Refrigerate for 45 minutes, until chocolate is set.

6. Break into small, irregular pieces. Store in an airtight container in the refrigerator or freezer.

Pomegranate Almond Chocolate Bark

pareve | passover | gluten-free | yields 8 servings

Ingredients

1 bar (14 oz/400 g) semisweet chocolate, broken into chunks

1 cup pomegranate seeds, divided

1 cup slivered almonds, divided

Method

1. Line a baking sheet with parchment paper.

2. Pour about 1 inch of water into a saucepan. Bring to a boil; reduce heat to a simmer.

3. Place chocolate into a large, dry, heatproof bowl wider than the saucepan. Place bowl over simmering water. Melt chocolate, stirring often.

4. Stir half the pomegranate seeds and half the almonds into melted chocolate. Pour mixture onto prepared pan; spread evenly. Sprinkle with remaining pomegranate seeds and almonds; press gently into chocolate.

5. Refrigerate for 45 minutes, until chocolate is set.

6. Break into small, irregular pieces. Store in an airtight container in the refrigerator or freezer.

Norene's Notes

- Never cover chocolate while melting it. The condensation that forms on the cover can cause the chocolate to seize (become clumpy and lumpy) if a drop or two of condensation falls into the chocolate. When melting chocolate, always make sure that the bowl and spoon are completely dry.

- Chocolate stored above 70°F will "bloom" (develop white streaks). The streaks will disappear when the chocolate melts.

White Chocolate Pretzel Bark

pareve | gluten-free option | yields 8 servings

Ingredients

1 bar (14 oz/400 g) semisweet chocolate, broken into chunks

1½ cups pretzels, salted or unsalted, coarsely chopped (regular or gluten-free), divided

½ cup white chocolate chips, divided

Method

1. Line a baking sheet with parchment paper.

2. Pour about 1 inch of water into a saucepan. Bring to a boil; reduce heat to a simmer.

3. Place chocolate into a large, dry, heatproof bowl wider than the saucepan. Place bowl over simmering water. Melt chocolate, stirring often. Cool slightly.

4. Stir half the pretzels and half the white chocolate chips into melted chocolate. Pour mixture onto prepared pan; spread evenly. Sprinkle with remaining pretzels and white chocolate chips; press gently into chocolate.

5. Refrigerate for 45 minutes, until chocolate is set.

6. Break into small, irregular pieces. Store in an airtight container in the refrigerator or freezer.

Trail Mix Chocolate Bark

pareve | gluten-free | yields 8 servings

Ingredients

1 bar (14 oz/400 g) semisweet chocolate, broken into chunks

1 cup dried cranberries

1 cup pumpkin seeds

1 cup sunflower seeds

Method

1. Line a baking sheet with parchment paper.

2. Pour about 1 inch of water into a saucepan. Bring to a boil; reduce heat to a simmer.

3. Place chocolate into a large, dry, heatproof bowl wider than the saucepan. Place bowl over simmering water. Melt chocolate, stirring often.

4. In a medium bowl, combine dried cranberries, pumpkin seeds, and sunflower seeds.

5. Stir about half the seed mixture into melted chocolate. Pour chocolate mixture onto prepared pan; spread evenly. Sprinkle with remaining seed mixture; press gently into chocolate.

6. Refrigerate for 45 minutes, until chocolate is set.

7. Break into small, irregular pieces. Store in an airtight container in the refrigerator or freezer.

Inspired by my Bubbie Mena Glustein, these candy-coated nuts are a staple in my kitchen. They're perfect as a pre-dinner sweet and crunchy snack, and also make a great addition to salads, sides, and desserts.

Candied Cinnamon Nuts

pareve | passover | gluten-free | freezes well | yields 3 cups

Ingredients

¼ cup water

1 cup sugar

2 tsp ground cinnamon

3 cups whole or slivered almonds or pecan halves

Method

1. Line a baking sheet with parchment paper. Set aside.

2. In a medium saucepan, combine water, sugar, and cinnamon; bring to a boil over medium heat.

3. Add nuts; cook and stir until all the liquid has evaporated. The coated nuts will turn a deep golden brown.

4. Pour onto prepared baking sheet. Spread into a single layer. Let cool completely. Break apart any clusters.

5. Store in an airtight container. Nuts will stay fresh for about 2 weeks.

Norene's Notes

- This recipe can be made with mixed nuts, hazelnuts, cashews, or walnuts, etc. The choice is yours.
- For a terrific topping for salads, coarsely chop Candied Cinnamon Nuts and sprinkle on salad.

Laughably easy to make, these rich, chocolate-dunked potato chips pack a salty-sweet punch that's completely irresistible. With only three ingredients and three prep steps (melt, dunk, cool), it's a truly eureka-worthy treat.

Chocolate-Dipped Chips

pareve | passover | gluten-free | freezes well | yields 6 servings

Ingredients

1½ cups chocolate chips

1 tsp vegetable oil

8 cups potato chips (ridged or regular)

Method

1. Line two baking sheets with parchment paper.

2. Pour about 1 inch of water into a saucepan. Bring to a boil; reduce heat to a simmer.

3. Place chocolate chips into a large, dry, heatproof bowl that is wider then the saucepan. Place bowl over simmering water. Slowly melt chocolate, stirring often. Stir in oil.

4. Dunk each potato chip halfway into chocolate, letting excess drip off. Place chips onto prepared pan in a single layer.

5. Refrigerate for 15 minutes or until chocolate is set.

6. Store in an airtight container in the refrigerator or freezer.

Norene's Notes

- Variation: Melt ½ cup white chocolate chips. Transfer to a piping bag and drizzle over chocolate-covered chips. No piping bag? Use a resealable plastic bag and snip a small piece from the corner.

- Chocolate-Dipped Banana Slices: Cut large, firm, peeled bananas into slices about half an inch thick. Dunk slices halfway into melted chocolate; refrigerate until set. For a fun look, use a crinkled cutter.

Satisfy your sweet tooth with this simple, no-bake treat. It's an easy way to get in those crunches. Great for a crowd!

White Chocolate Popcorn Clusters

pareve | gluten-free | freezes well | yields 8-10 servings

Ingredients

2½ cups white chocolate chips

8 cups popped popcorn (salted or unsalted)

1 cup dried cranberries

Method

1. Line a baking sheet with parchment paper.

2. Pour about 1 inch of water into a saucepan. Bring to a boil; reduce heat to a simmer.

3. Place chocolate into a large, dry, heatproof bowl wider than the saucepan. Place bowl over simmering water. Slowly melt chocolate, stirring often.

4. Add popcorn; stir until coated. Fold in cranberries. Use a large cookie scoop or large spoon to drop mixture onto parchment paper, making small clusters.

5. Refrigerate for at least 45 minutes or until completely firm. Store in an airtight container in the refrigerator or freezer.

Norene's Notes

• To avoid a future trip to the dentist, make sure to use only the popcorn kernels that have popped!

These salty, sweet treats are perfect for those times when an entire cake seems too formal, but you don't want guests to leave without dessert. Fun, bright, and bite-sized, these are always a huge hit!

Rainbow Pretzels

pareve | gluten-free option | freezes well | yields about 30-40 pretzels

Ingredients

1 bar (14 oz/400 g) semisweet chocolate, broken into chunks

1 pkg (14 oz/400 g) pretzels, salted or unsalted (regular or gluten-free)

3 cups rainbow sprinkles

Method

1. Line 2 baking sheets with parchment paper.

2. Pour about 1 inch of water into a saucepan. Bring to a boil; reduce heat to a simmer.

3. Place chocolate into a large, dry, heatproof bowl wider than the saucepan. Place bowl over simmering water. Slowly melt chocolate, stirring often.

4. Make an assembly line with bowls of whole pretzels, melted chocolate, and sprinkles.

5. Dunk each pretzel halfway into chocolate, letting excess drip off. Then dip into sprinkles, coating both sides. Place onto baking sheet. Repeat until all pretzels and/or chocolate have been used.

6. Refrigerate for 15 minutes or until chocolate is set.

7. Store in an airtight container in the refrigerator or freezer.

Norene's Notes

- You can substitute 2½ cups chocolate chips for the chocolate bar. Stir 1 tsp oil into the melted chocolate for a lovely shine.
- Save any leftover broken pretzels in a resealable bag. You can crush them to use as a coating for chicken or fish (but don't use the chocolate-coated ones!).
- Bittersweet and semisweet chocolate are interchangeable. The darker the chocolate, the higher the antioxidant content and the lower the sugar content.

This is such a beautifully presented dish. It's amazing that one color can be so different in texture and taste. These fresh fruits taste even fresher when you add mint, resulting in a perfect dessert for a hot summer day.

The Green Fruit Salad

pareve | passover | gluten-free | do not freeze | yields 8 servings

Ingredients

3 cups seedless green grapes

3 green apples, cored and diced (do not peel)

3 kiwis, peeled and diced

½ honeydew, scooped into balls

zest and juice of **2** limes

2-3 Tbsp honey

fresh mint leaves, for garnish

Method

1. Rinse grapes and dry well. Remove and discard any stems. Place grapes into a resealable plastic bag; place into freezer for at least 2 hours or overnight.

2. In a large bowl, combine apples, kiwis, and honeydew. Stir in lime zest, juice, and honey; toss to combine. Cover and refrigerate.

3. Just before serving, add frozen grapes.

4. Spoon fruit salad into individual parfait glasses or bowls. Add a mint leaf for garnish.

Norene's Notes

- Although the assembled fruit salad shouldn't be frozen, the leftover fruit certainly can be. Store leftover fruit in the freezer in resealable bags and use for smoothies.
- Variation: Make Fruit Popsicles by combining 4 cups cut-up fruit in a mixing bowl and spooning fruit into popsicle molds. Pour in enough lemonade (about 2 cups in total) to just cover the fruit. Insert popsicle sticks; freeze overnight. Cool!

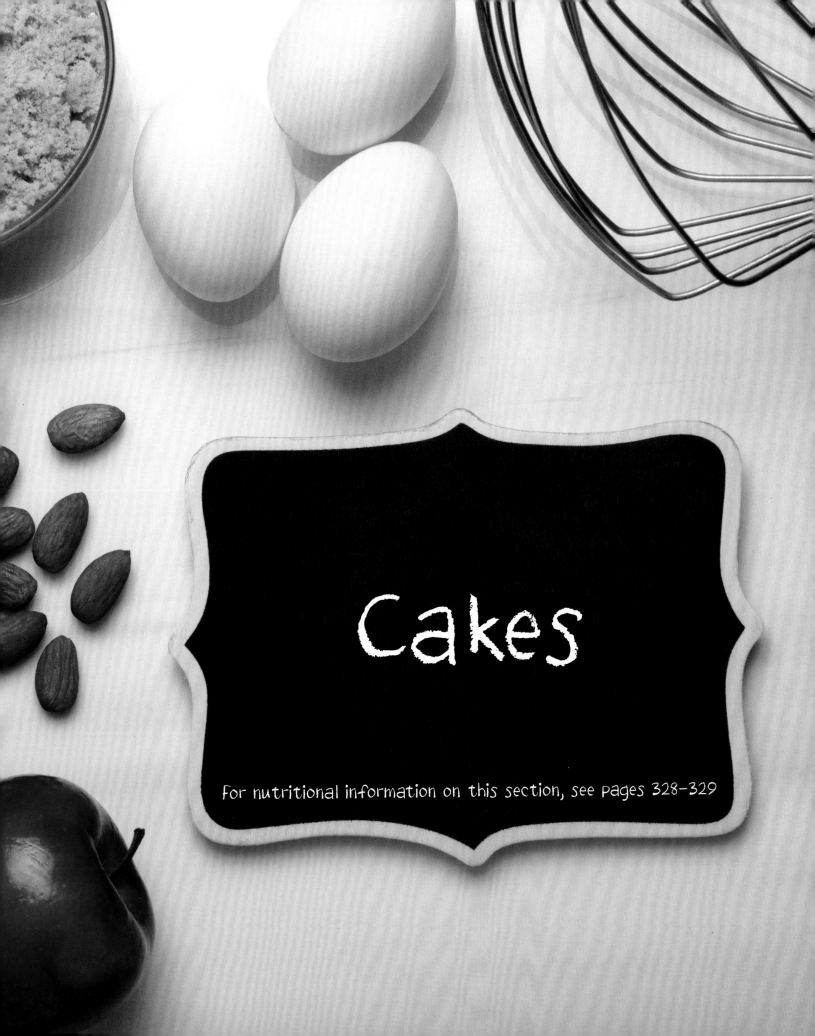

Cakes

For nutritional information on this section, see pages 328–329

This apple-studded cake creates a feeling of warmth that symbolizes the taste of home. Dress it up for company with a scoop of ice cream or make into apple muffins for a quick breakfast on the go (see Norene's Notes, below).

Apple Cinnamon Cake

pareve | gluten-free option | freezes well | yields 12-15 servings

Ingredients

Filling

6 large apples (e.g., Cortland, Honeycrisp, or Granny Smith), cored, peeled, quartered, and thinly sliced

1 Tbsp ground cinnamon

1 Tbsp sugar

1 Tbsp flour (or gluten-free flour with xanthan gum)

Batter

4 eggs

1¾ cups sugar

1 cup vegetable oil

2 tsp pure vanilla extract

2¾ cups flour (or gluten-free flour with xanthan gum)

3 tsp baking powder

¼ tsp salt

1 tsp ground cinnamon

¼ cup apple juice

confectioner's sugar, for dusting

Method

1. Preheat oven to 350°F. Coat a 12-cup Bundt pan or 9 x 13-inch baking pan with nonstick spray.

2. **Filling:** In a large bowl, combine all filling ingredients. Toss to combine.

3. **Batter:** In the large bowl of an electric mixer fitted with the paddle attachment, beat eggs with sugar, oil, and vanilla on medium-high speed for 3-5 minutes, until light.

4. In a medium bowl, combine flour, baking powder, salt, and cinnamon. Stir to combine.

5. Reduce mixer speed to low. Add half of flour mixture; then blend in juice, followed by remaining flour mixture. Use a rubber spatula to fold in apples.

6. Pour batter into prepared pan; spread evenly.

7. Bake about 1 hour and 15 minutes if using a Bundt pan or 1 hour if using a 9 x 13-inch pan. A wooden toothpick inserted into the center should come out without any batter clinging to it.

8. Allow cake to cool for 20 minutes. Invert Bundt cake onto serving platter. Leave 9 x 13-inch cake in pan. Dust cake with confectioner's sugar when cool.

Norene's Notes

- If frozen and defrosted, cake will become very moist; reheat, uncovered, at 350°F for 15-20 minutes.
- Apple Cinnamon Muffins: Prepare batter as directed above; scoop batter into muffin pans lined with paper liners. Fill compartments two-thirds full. Bake at 375°F for 25-30 minutes, until nicely browned. Makes about 2 dozen muffins.

My mom, Resa Litwack, still makes this recipe for us today. When time is tight, I always turn to this moist, delicious, no-fail cake. The cake is versatile enough to work for Shabbat breakfast or as a homey dessert.

Banana Chocolate Chip Cake

pareve | gluten-free option | freezes well | yields 10-12 servings

Ingredients

2 eggs

1 cup brown sugar, packed

½ cup vegetable oil

1 tsp pure vanilla extract

2 large, very ripe mashed bananas (about 1 cup)

2 cups flour (or gluten-free flour with xanthan gum)

1 tsp baking powder

1 tsp baking soda

pinch salt

¾ cup orange juice

1 cup chocolate chips (see Norene's Notes, below)

Method

1. Preheat oven 350°F. Coat a 7 x 11-inch glass baking dish with nonstick spray.

2. In the bowl of an electric mixer fitted with the paddle attachement, beat eggs with brown sugar, oil, and vanilla on medium-high speed for 3-5 minutes, until light. Add mashed bananas; mix just until blended.

3. In a medium bowl, combine flour, baking powder, baking soda, and salt.

4. Reduce mixer speed to low. Add dry ingredients alternately with orange juice, mixing just until blended. Fold in chocolate chips.

5. Bake 35-40 minutes or until a wooden toothpick inserted into the center comes out clean.

Norene's Notes

- Variations: Instead of orange juice, combine 2 tsp lemon juice plus enough soy or rice milk to equal ½ cup. Instead of chocolate chips, substitute fresh or frozen blueberries (no need to thaw them first).

- Banana Muffins: Prepare batter as directed above. Line muffin pans or mini muffin pans with paper cupcake liners. Fill compartments two-thirds full. Bake muffins at 350°F for 22-25 minutes or minis for 12-15 minutes, until golden. Makes 12-15 muffins or 36 minis.

Carrot cake always offers a warm, welcome-home feeling. Layered with a creamy frosting and topped with shredded coconut, this cake is a taste of heaven.

Carrot Cake
with coconut topping

dairy | pareve option | gluten-free option | freezes well | yields 10-12 servings

Ingredients

4 eggs

1½ cups sugar

1½ cups vegetable oil

1 tsp pure vanilla extract

3 cups grated carrots, (about 6 carrots)

2 cups flour (or gluten-free flour with xanthan gum)

2 tsp baking powder

1 tsp baking soda

1 Tbsp ground cinnamon

½ tsp kosher salt

Cream Cheese Frosting

1 cup cream cheese

½ cup butter

1 Tbsp lemon juice

4 cups confectioner's sugar

1 cup flaked or shredded unsweetened coconut

Method

1. Preheat oven to 350°F. Line the bottom of two 9- or 10-inch cake pans with parchment paper; coat with nonstick cooking spray.

2. In the bowl of an electric mixer fitted with the paddle attachment, beat eggs with sugar, oil, and vanilla on medium-high speed about 3-5 minutes, until light. Add carrots; mix well.

3. In a medium bowl, combine flour, baking powder, baking soda, cinnamon, and salt. Stir to combine.

4. Reduce mixer speed to low. Add flour mixture; mix just until combined.

5. Divide batter evenly between pans. Bake 30-35 minutes, or until a toothpick inserted into the center comes out clean. Cool completely.

6. **Frosting:** In the bowl of an electric mixer, beat cream cheese, butter, and lemon juice on medium-high speed until creamy. Reduce speed to low; gradually add confectioner's sugar, beating until smooth.

7. Run a knife around the edge of pans to loosen each cake. Invert one layer onto a round serving platter. Remove and discard parchment paper. Using a flexible spatula, spread a layer of frosting over cake layer.

8. Top with the second layer. Remove and discard parchment paper. Frost top of cake and sprinkle with coconut. Store, covered, in the refrigerator.

Norene's Notes

• Pareve option: Substitute Coconut "Whipped Cream" for Cream Cheese Frosting. Chill 2 cans (14 oz/398 ml each) organic unsweetened full-fat coconut milk overnight. Open cans from the bottom; pour off coconut liquid (save for smoothies). Whip thickened coconut cream in a chilled bowl until light. Blend in ¼ cup confectioner's sugar and 1 tsp vanilla. Spread on cake.

My friend Chayala Bistricer often makes this beautiful cake for Shabbat. For an added garnish, she sprinkles candied nuts around the cake. If you have nut allergies, garnish with berries, mint leaves, or parve whipped cream.

Flourless Chocolate Mousse Cake

pareve | passover | gluten-free | freezes well | yields 12 servings

Ingredients

8 oz/250 g semisweet chocolate or chocolate chips

½ cup vegetable oil

2 tsp pure vanilla extract

8 eggs, separated

1 cup sugar, divided

Method

1. Preheat oven to 325°F. Coat a 9- or 10-inch springform pan with nonstick cooking spray.

2. Combine chocolate, oil, and vanilla in a medium saucepan over low heat. Melt chocolate, stirring often. Cool to lukewarm.

3. In an electric mixer fitted with the paddle attachment, beat egg yolks on high speed for 3-5 minutes. Gradually add ½ cup sugar; continue beating until light. Add yolk mixture to cooled chocolate; mix well.

4. Wash and dry beaters and bowl. Fit mixer with whisk attachment. Place egg whites into bowl; beat on medium speed for 3-5 minutes, until frothy. Increase speed to high; gradually add remaining sugar. Beat until stiff.

5. Fold batter into meringue, just until no traces of white remain.

6. Pour three-quarters of batter into prepared pan; spread evenly, using a rubber spatula. Cover and refrigerate remaining batter. (See Norene's Notes, below.) Bake 30-35 minutes, until top of cake is set when touched lightly with your fingertips. Cool completely. The cake will sink somewhat.

7. Stir refrigerated batter to soften it slightly. Spread evenly over top of cake. Cover pan tightly with foil; freeze.

8. Before serving, transfer cake to a flat round platter and remove sides of springform pan.

Norene's Notes

- Safety Note: The batter used as a topping contains uncooked eggs. If desired, bake the entire batter, increasing baking time by 10-15 minutes.
- See Egg White Wisdom (p. 268) for more on whipping egg whites properly.

There's something blissfully nostalgic about rocky road brownies. This cake is beyond delicious, with its chocolate drizzle and puffs of fluffy marshmallow. It's also perfect for Passover.

Rocky Road Brownie Cake

pareve | passover | gluten-free | freezes well | yields 12-24 servings

Ingredients

4 eggs

1¾ cups sugar

1 cup vegetable oil

1 cup potato starch

¾ cup unsweetened cocoa powder

pinch kosher salt

3 cups mini marshmallows

½ cup chocolate chips

Method

1. Preheat oven to 350°F. Lightly coat bottom and sides of a 9- or 10-inch springform pan with nonstick cooking spray. (Alternatively, use a 9 x 13-inch glass baking dish; see Norene's Notes, below.)

2. In a large bowl, combine eggs, sugar, and oil; mix until well blended.

3. Add potato starch, cocoa, and salt; mix until combined.

4. Pour batter into prepared pan; spread evenly.

5. Bake 35-40 minutes. Remove pan from oven and sprinkle evenly with marshmallows. Bake an additional 5 minutes, until marshmallows are puffed and slightly golden.

6. Let cool. Melt chocolate chips; drizzle melted chocolate in a zigzag design over marshmallows. Transfer to a round serving plate; remove sides from springform pan. Cut into 12 wedges.

Norene's Notes

- If using a 9 x 13-inch pan, line with aluminum foil, with ends of foil extending over sides of pan. Use foil handles to lift baked, cooled brownies from pan before cutting into 24 squares.
- Variation: In step 5, add ¾ cup coarsely chopped pecans and ¾ cup shredded unsweetened coconut along with marshmallows.
- It's better to underbake brownies slightly. If they are overbaked, they will taste dry and crumbly rather than rich and moist. If you took your brownies out of the oven too early and they seem slightly underbaked, place the entire pan of brownies into the refrigerator and they will become moist and fudgy.

This isn't your average coffee-time cake! Vanilla and chocolate glazes drizzled over the top let you see the marbling of the cake peeking out.

Double-Glazed Marble Cake

pareve | gluten-free option | unglazed cake freezes well | yields 12 servings

Ingredients

3 eggs

1¼ cups sugar

1¼ cups vegetable oil

2 tsp pure vanilla extract

1½ cups soy or rice milk

2½ cups flour (or gluten-free flour with xanthan gum)

1 tsp baking powder

1½ tsp baking soda

¼ cup melted semisweet chocolate chips

White Glaze

1 cup confectioner's sugar

2 Tbsp soy or rice milk

Chocolate Glaze

1 cup confectioner's sugar

3 Tbsp cocoa

3-4 Tbsp hot water

Method

1. Preheat oven to 350°F. Coat a 12-cup Bundt pan with nonstick cooking spray.

2. Combine eggs, sugar, oil, and vanilla in the large bowl of an electric mixer fitted with the paddle attachment. Beat on medium-high speed for 3-5 minutes, until light. Add soy milk; mix well.

3. Reduce mixer speed to low; add in flour, baking powder, and baking soda; mix just until combined.

4. Pour two-thirds of batter into prepared pan. Add melted chocolate chips to remaining batter and mix briefly, just until blended.

5. Drizzle chocolate batter over white batter. Cut through batters in a swirl design with a knife or spatula.

6. Bake for 45-50 minutes, until a wooden toothpick inserted into center comes out clean.

7. Let cool 20 minutes. Unmold cake onto a serving platter. Cool completely before glazing.

8. **White Glaze:** In a medium bowl, combine confectioner's sugar with soy milk; stir until blended. Drizzle white glaze over cooled cake.

9. **Chocolate Glaze:** In a medium bowl, combine confectioner's sugar with cocoa and water; stir until blended. Drizzle chocolate glaze over white glaze, forming a striped effect.

Norene's Notes

• If you freeze the cake, do so before glazing; glaze may crack if frozen.

This scrumptious cake is a winner. The kids love the chocolate chip surprise, and the fresh berries keep it colorful. It's light, fun, and presents beautifully — the perfect cake for a relaxed afternoon with company.

Chocolate Chip Berry Cake

pareve | gluten-free option | freezes well | yields 12 servings

Ingredients

3 eggs

1 cup sugar

⅔ cup vegetable oil

2 tsp pure vanilla extract

3 cups flour (or gluten-free flour with xanthan gum)

3 tsp baking powder

1 tsp baking soda

¼ tsp salt

1½ cups orange juice

3 cups assorted fresh berries

1 cup chocolate chips

1 Tbsp flour (or gluten-free flour with xanthan gum)

Topping

¾ cup flour (or gluten-free flour with xanthan gum)

½ cup sugar

1½ tsp ground cinnamon

¼ cup vegetable oil

confectioner's sugar, for sprinkling

Method

1. Preheat oven to 350°F. Line bottom of a 10- or 12-inch tube pan with a round of parchment paper. Coat sides of pan with nonstick cooking spray.

2. In the bowl of an electric mixer fitted with the paddle attachment, beat eggs with sugar, oil, and vanilla on medium-high speed for 3-5 minutes, until light. Reduce mixer speed to low.

3. Combine flour, baking powder, baking soda, and salt in a medium bowl; add to mixture alternately with orange juice, starting and ending with dry ingredients.

4. Combine berries, chocolate chips, and 1 tablespoon flour in a medium bowl; toss to combine. Using a rubber spatula, fold mixture thoroughly into batter. Pour batter into prepared pan; spread evenly.

5. **Topping:** In the same bowl used for the berry mixture, stir together flour, sugar, cinnamon, and oil, forming a crumbly topping. Sprinkle topping evenly over batter.

6. Bake for 60-65 minutes, or until a wooden toothpick inserted into the center comes out clean. (Some berries may cling to the toothpick.)

7. Allow cake to cool. Invert cake onto a large plate; carefully invert onto a serving platter so topping is on top. Dust with confectioner's sugar.

Norene's Notes

- How do you know if baking powder is still fresh? Dissolve ½ tsp of baking powder in ½ cup of hot water. If it fizzes, it's fine. Average shelf life of baking powder is about one year.

A huge hit with adults and kids alike, this simple cake is mixed with chopped-up sandwich cookies, adding a crunchy, gooey element to the moist cake. Thanks to my mom, Resa Litwack, for always making this family favorite for us!

Cookie Cake

pareve | gluten-free option | freezes well | yields 12 servings

Ingredients

3 eggs

1½ cups sugar

1¼ cups vegetable oil

2 tsp pure vanilla extract

1½ cups orange juice

2½ cups flour (or gluten-free flour with xanthan gum)

1 tsp baking powder

1½ tsp baking soda

pinch salt

4 cups coarsely chopped chocolate sandwich cookies (gluten-free or regular)

1 cup chocolate chips

Method

1. Preheat oven to 350°F. Coat a 12-cup Bundt pan with nonstick cooking spray.

2. In the bowl of an electric mixer fitted with the paddle attachment, beat eggs with sugar, oil, and vanilla on medium-high speed for 3-5 minutes, until light. Add orange juice; beat well.

3. Reduce mixer speed to low; add flour, baking powder, baking soda, and salt. Mix just until combined.

4. Carefully fold in cookies and chocolate chips. Pour batter into prepared pan.

5. Bake for 50-55 minutes or until a wooden toothpick inserted into the center comes out without any batter clinging to it.

6. Let cool 20 minutes. Invert onto a serving platter; cool completely.

Norene's Notes

• To chop the cookies easily, place them into a large resealable bag. Smash them with a rolling pin until coarsely chopped. (Kids can help with this task.) Do not crush them too finely or you will end up with crumbs!

• You can also use a 9 x 13-inch baking pan coated with nonstick cooking spray.

This gorgeous glazed honey cake, using only one tablespoon of oil, makes a spectacular dessert. The recipe was inspired by my wonderful Bubbie, Noreen Lax. The pretty glaze adds an extra-special, festive feel.

Pomegranate-Glazed Honey Cake

pareve | gluten-free option | unglazed cake freezes well | yields 12-15 servings

Ingredients

3 eggs

1 cup sugar

1 Tbsp vegetable oil

1 cup water

2 Tbsp instant coffee granules

1 cup honey

2⅔ cups flour (or gluten-free flour with xantham gum)

2 tsp baking powder

1 tsp baking soda

1 tsp cinnamon

Glaze

1½ cups confectioner's sugar

3 Tbsp pomegranate juice

Method

1. Preheat oven to 325°F. Coat a 12-cup Bundt or 10-inch tube pan with nonstick cooking spray.

2. In the bowl of an electric mixer fitted with the paddle attachment, beat eggs, sugar, and oil on medium-high speed for 3-5 minutes, until light. Add water, coffee, and honey; mix well.

3. Reduce mixer speed to low. Add flour, baking powder, baking soda, and cinnamon. Mix just until combined.

4. Pour batter into prepared pan and spread evenly.

5. Bake about 1 hour, or until a wooden toothpick inserted into the center comes out clean.

6. Let cool 20 minutes. Carefully invert cake onto a large serving platter; cool completely before glazing.

7. **Glaze:** In a medium bowl, whisk together confectioner's sugar and pomegranate juice.

8. Drizzle glaze over cooled cake, allowing it to run down the sides.

Norene's Notes

• If you freeze the baked cake, glaze it after defrosting. Glaze may crack if frozen.

• Variation: Divide batter among three 8 x 4-inch loaf pans; bake at 325°F for 45-50 minutes. If using disposable foil pans, place them on a baking sheet for even heat conduction. Great for gift-giving!

Rich, easy, and elegant, this no-fail chocolate tart is one of my favorite gluten-free desserts. The rustic almond crust gives the tart a crunchy contrast of textures and the nutty flavor pairs beautifully with the creamy, rich chocolate ganache.

Almond-Crusted Chocolate Tart

pareve | passover | dairy option | gluten-free | freezes well | yields 10 servings

Ingredients

Crust

1½ cups almond meal flour

½ tsp ground cinnamon

pinch kosher salt

¼ cup vegetable oil

¼ cup brown sugar, lightly packed

½ tsp pure vanilla extract

Ganache Filling

1¼ cups nondairy whipping cream

1 bar (10 oz/300 g) semisweet chocolate, chopped

Topping

1 cup toasted slivered almonds

½ cup chocolate chips, melted

Method

1. Preheat oven to 325°F. Coat bottom and sides of a 9-inch glass pie plate or a tart pan with removable bottom with nonstick cooking spray.

2. **Crust:** Combine almond flour, cinnamon, and salt in a large bowl. Add oil, sugar, and vanilla; stir to combine. Pat evenly into bottom and up the sides of prepared pan, forming a crust.

3. Bake about 25 minutes, until golden and set. Let cool.

4. **Ganache Filling:** In a medium saucepan, bring cream to a boil over medium-high heat. Remove pan from heat. Add chocolate and stir until melted.

5. Pour chocolate ganache into cooled crust. Let set for 10 minutes.

6. **Topping:** Sprinkle with toasted almonds and drizzle with melted chocolate in a zigzag design. Refrigerate for 4 hours or overnight. Serve chilled.

Norene's Notes

- Variation: For a dairy version, replace Ganache Filling with the following filling: Whip together 1 cup (8 oz/250 g) cream cheese, ½ cup confectioner's sugar, ½ tsp pure vanilla extract and 2 Tbsp milk until well blended. Spread over crust. Top with 2 cups sliced strawberries and melted chocolate.

- Almond meal flour is made from skinless blanched almonds that have been finely ground.

This elegant flan was inspired by my mother-in-law, Bonny Silver — it's a family favorite! This is best made in blueberry season, when local berries are fresh, plentiful, and inexpensive.

Blueberry Flan

pareve | gluten-free option | do not freeze | yields 10 servings

Ingredients

Dough

1½ cups flour (or gluten-free flour with xanthan gum)

¼ cup sugar

1 tsp ground cinnamon

¾ cup vegetable oil

1½ Tbsp vinegar

Filling

6 cups blueberries, divided

½ cup sugar

2 Tbsp flour (or gluten-free flour with xanthan gum)

1 tsp ground cinnamon

confectioner's sugar, for garnish

Method

1. Preheat oven to 375°F. Lightly coat an 11-inch flan pan or pie plate with removable bottom with nonstick cooking spray.

2. **Dough:** In a large bowl, combine flour, sugar, and cinnamon. Add oil and vinegar; mix together to make a soft dough.

3. Press dough evenly against bottom and sides of prepared pan.

4. **Filling:** In a large bowl, combine 5 cups blueberries, sugar, flour, and cinnamon. Stir gently to combine. Spoon filling into crust.

5. Bake 50-60 minutes, or until blueberries have popped. Let cool.

6. Before serving, top flan with reserved blueberries and dust with confectioner's sugar.

Norene's Notes

• When fresh blueberries aren't in season, frozen berries work well for the filling, as they are less expensive and just as tasty. However, it's best to use fresh berries for the top.

Rustic, fun, and perfect for summer, this crumble is a great dessert for any occasion. Serve it warm with a scoop of vanilla ice cream on the side.

Cranberry-Blueberry Crumble

pareve | gluten-free option | freezes well | yields 8 servings

Ingredients

Filling

2 cups cranberries (fresh or frozen)

4 cups blueberries (fresh or frozen)

⅓ cup brown sugar, lightly packed

1 tsp ground cinnamon

⅓ cup flour

Topping

1 cup flour (or gluten-free flour with xanthan gum)

1 cup rolled oats

½ cup brown sugar, lightly packed

2 tsp ground cinnamon

⅓ cup vegetable oil

Method

1. Preheat oven to 350°F. Coat 8 ramekins or a 10-inch deep pie plate with nonstick cooking spray and place onto a parchment-lined rimmed baking sheet.

2. **Filling:** In a medium bowl, combine cranberries, blueberries, sugar, cinnamon, and flour. Mix well.

3. **Topping:** In a second bowl, combine topping ingredients; mix together to form crumbs.

4. Divide filling among ramekins or spoon into pie plate. Sprinkle evenly with topping mixture.

5. Bake ramekins for 35-40 minutes or large crumble for 45-55 minutes, until topping is golden and juices are bubbly. Serve warm or at room temperature.

Norene's Notes

- If crumble has been frozen, reheat before serving to crisp up topping.
- Variation: Instead of cranberries, substitute nectarines. Instead of blueberries, substitute strawberries.
- Do-Ahead: Assemble crumbles earlier in the day and store them in the refrigerator. Bake before dinner.

This is a classic cheesecake — Israel-style. Crumbled into the cream cheese mixture, halvah adds a nutty flavor and feathery texture that make this dessert truly divine.

Heavenly Halvah Cheesecake

dairy | passover option | gluten-free option | freezes well | yields 10 servings

Ingredients

Crust

1½ cups finely ground graham crackers (gluten-free or regular) (about 18-24 crackers)

⅓ cup melted butter

2 Tbsp brown sugar

Filling

4 pkgs (8 oz/250 g each) cream cheese, room temperature

1⅓ cups sugar

4 eggs

2 tsp pure vanilla extract

1 cup crumbled halvah (white or marbled)

additional crumbled halvah for garnish (about ¾-1 cup)

Method

1. Preheat oven to 350°F. Coat bottom and sides of a 9- or 10-inch springform pan with nonstick cooking spray.

2. **Crust:** In a bowl, combine cracker crumbs with butter and sugar; mix well. Press crumb mixture evenly into bottom of prepared pan.

3. **Filling:** In the bowl of an electric mixer fitted with the paddle attachment or in a food processor, beat cream cheese and sugar until light. Add eggs and vanilla; beat until smooth and creamy, scraping down sides of bowl as needed. Using a rubber spatula, fold in 1 cup crumbled halvah.

4. Pour filling over crust; spread evenly.

5. Fill a pie plate halfway with water; place on lowest oven rack. Place cheesecake on middle rack. Bake for 40-45 minutes. When done, edges will be set, but the center 2 inches will jiggle slightly. Don't overbake.

6. Turn off heat, prop oven door partially open with a wooden spoon, and let cheesecake cool in oven for 1 hour to finish baking and firm up.

7. Refrigerate for several hours or overnight before serving. Garnish with additional crumbled halvah.

Norene's Notes

- The pan of water on the lowest oven rack creates steam during baking, resulting in a cheesecake with a creamy, scrumptious texture.
- Don't overbake cheesecake; the top will crack if baked until the center is set.
- Passover Variation: Omit halvah from filling and topping. Replace graham wafers with crushed Passover cookies. Top baked cheesecake with four cups hulled sliced or whole strawberries. Brush with ½ cup melted apricot jam.

"Nutrition is all about balance and variety, so don't be afraid to mix it up!"

Nutritional Information

The nutritional analysis was calculated using data from ESHA (The Food Processor SQL Edition 10.14.2) and, when necessary, manufacturers' food labels.

- When a recipe indicates a range of servings (4-6 servings), it was analyzed for 4 servings.

- When there is a choice of ingredients, the first ingredient was analyzed. The analysis does not include optional ingredients or those with no specified amounts.

- The smaller measure of an ingredient was analyzed when a range is given (e.g., ¼ cup was analyzed when a recipe calls for ¼-⅓ cup).

- The nutrient values have been rounded off for carbohydrates, fiber, fat, calories, protein, cholesterol, sodium, potassium, iron, calcium, and phosphorus.

- The phosphorus content included in the analysis is helpful for people with medical problems, including kidney disease.

- A serving of at least 2 grams of fiber is considered a moderate source, 4 grams is a high source, and 6 grams is considered a very high source of fiber.

- When eggs are called for, the recipe was analyzed using large eggs.

- Specific measurements of salt were included in the analysis (e.g., 1 tsp salt). When a recipe does not give a specific measurement (e.g., salt to taste), then salt was not included in the analysis. To reduce sodium content, choose low-sodium or salt-free products. Note that sodium content varies by brand of soy or tamari sauce; the sodium content of your dish may vary from the amount listed in this directory.

- When cheese is called for, the recipe was analyzed using lower fat or reduced fat cheeses, unless otherwise indicated.

- When sour cream or yogurt is called for, the recipe was analyzed using lower fat versions, unless otherwise indicated.

- When milk is called for, the recipe was analyzed using 1% milk, unless otherwise indicated.

- Garnishes were not calculated, unless a specific amount is indicated.

- To keep your recipes gluten-free, use gluten-free soy sauce or tamari.

- To keep your recipes dairy-free, use rice, soy, unsweetened almond, or coconut milk.

APPETIZERS

ASIAN-STYLE RICE PAPER ROLLS *p. 12*
(including dipping sauce)
Calories: 165 kcal
Carbs: 21 g (7 g sugar, 5 g of fiber)
Protein: 5 g
Fat: 8 g (1 g saturated)
Cholesterol: 0 mg
Potassium: 439 mg
Phosphorus: 36 mg
Calcium: 34 mg
Sodium: 638 mg
Iron: 1 mg

BABY EGGPLANT FANS *p. 22*
Calories: 176 kcal
Carbs: 14 g (2 g sugar, 5 g of fiber)
Protein: 7 g
Fat: 11 g (2 g saturated)
Cholesterol: 0 mg
Potassium: 223 mg
Phosphorus: 117 mg
Calcium: 30 mg
Sodium: 843 mg
Iron: 2 mg

BAKED VEGETABLE EGG ROLLS *p. 16*
(Serving size: 1 roll, including sauce)
Calories: 147 kcal
Carbs: 26 g (5 g sugar, 3 g of fiber)
Protein: 5 g
Fat: 3 g (0 g saturated)
Cholesterol: 3 mg
Potassium: 81 mg
Phosphorus: 33 mg
Calcium: 39 mg
Sodium: 603 mg
Iron: 2 mg

CRUNCHY CORNED BEEF STRIPS *p. 36*
Calories: 233 kcal
Carbs: 11 g (11 g sugar, 0 g of fiber)
Protein: 14 g
Fat: 14 g (5 g saturated)
Cholesterol: 74 mg
Potassium: 115 mg
Phosphorus: 95 mg
Calcium: 7 mg
Sodium: 1138 mg
Iron: 1 mg

CRUNCHY GUACAMOLE *p. 24*
(Serving size: ¼ cup)
Calories: 88 kcal
Carbs: 6 g (1 g sugar, 4 g of fiber)
Protein: 1 g
Fat: 7 g (1 g saturated)
Cholesterol: 0 mg
Potassium: 307 mg
Phosphorus: 34 mg
Calcium: 12 mg
Sodium: 9 mg
Iron: 0 mg

FRESH SALMON PATTIES *p. 18*
(per patty)
Calories: 124 kcal
Carbs: 7 g (1 g sugar, 1 g of fiber)
Protein: 12 g
Fat: 5 g (1 g saturated)
Cholesterol: 62 mg
Potassium: 169 mg
Phosphorus: 127 mg
Calcium: 47 mg
Sodium: 387 mg
Iron: 1 mg

GARLIC-ROASTED LENTILS *p. 28*
(Serving size: ¼ cup)
Calories: 98 kcal
Carbs: 14 g (1 g sugar, 6 g of fiber)
Protein: 6 g
Fat: 2 g (0 g saturated)
Cholesterol: 0 mg
Potassium: 262 mg
Phosphorus: 127 mg
Calcium: 14 mg
Sodium: 242 mg
Iron: 2 mg

HERBED BALSAMIC WINGS *p. 32*
Calories: 290 kcal
Carbs: 7 g (7 g sugar, 0 g of fiber)
Protein: 25 g
Fat: 17 g (5 g saturated)
Cholesterol: 144 mg
Potassium: 253 mg
Phosphorus: 155 mg
Calcium: 29 mg
Sodium: 105 mg
Iron: 1 mg

HONEY-GARLIC MUSHROOMS & RICE *p. 14*
Calories: 251 kcal
Carbs: 42 g (12 g sugar, 3 g of fiber)
Protein: 6 g
Fat: 7 g (1 g saturated)
Cholesterol: 0 mg
Potassium: 403 mg
Phosphorus: 99 mg
Calcium: 25 mg
Sodium: 743 mg
Iron: 2 mg

HONEY-GLAZED WINGS *p. 33*
Calories: 345 kcal
Carbs: 22 g (21 g sugar, 0 g of fiber)
Protein: 25 g
Fat: 17 g (5 g saturated)
Cholesterol: 144 mg
Potassium: 236 mg
Phosphorus: 153 mg
Calcium: 22 mg
Sodium: 751 mg
Iron: 1 mg

ISRAELI-STYLE SATAY WITH TAHINI DIPPING SAUCE *p. 34*
Calories: 272 kcal
Carbs: 7 g (0 g sugar, 2 g of fiber)
Protein: 31 g
Fat: 14 g (2 g saturated)
Cholesterol: 73 mg
Potassium: 372 mg
Phosphorus: 366 mg
Calcium: 53 mg
Sodium: 234 mg
Iron: 2 mg

MINI MEATBALLS *p. 30*
Calories: 274 kcal
Carbs: 19 g (14 g sugar, 2 g of fiber)
Protein: 23 g
Fat: 13 g (5 g saturated)
Cholesterol: 71 mg
Potassium: 715 mg
Phosphorus: 225 mg
Calcium: 103 mg
Sodium: 570 mg
Iron: 5 mg

ROASTED ASPARAGUS WITH POACHED EGGS *p. 20*
Calories: 133 kcal
Carbs: 5 g (3 g sugar, 2 g of fiber)
Protein: 8 g
Fat: 9 g (2 g saturated)
Cholesterol: 187 mg
Potassium: 240 mg
Phosphorus: 128mg
Calcium: 44 mg
Sodium: 74 mg
Iron: 1 mg

ROASTED CORN NIBLETS *p. 29*
(Serving size: ¼ cup)
Calories: 170 kcal
Carbs: 29 g (9 g sugar, 2 g of fiber)
Protein: 4g
Fat: 4 g (0 g saturated)
Cholesterol: 0 mg
Potassium: 31 mg
Phosphorus: 4 mg
Calcium: 3 mg
Sodium: 791 mg
Iron: 0 mg

ROASTED EDAMAME BEANS *p. 29*
(Serving size: ¼ cup)
Calories: 85 kcal
Carbs: 5 g (2 g sugar, 3 g of fiber)
Protein: 6 g
Fat: 5 g (0 g saturated)
Cholesterol: 0 mg
Potassium: 301 mg
Phosphorus: 101 mg
Calcium: 38 mg
Sodium: 244 mg
Iron: 1 mg

ROASTED EGGPLANT DIP *p. 26*
(Serving size: ¼ cup)
Calories: 62 kcal
Carbs: 9 g (4 g sugar, 2 g of fiber)
Protein: 1 g
Fat: 3 g (0 g saturated)
Cholesterol: 0 mg
Potassium: 163 mg
Phosphorus: 18 mg
Calcium: 11 mg
Sodium: 12 mg
Iron: 0 mg

SPICY CHICKPEAS *p. 28*
(Serving size: ¼ cup)
Calories: 176 kcal
Carbs: 25 g (4 g sugar, 7 g of fiber)
Protein: 8 g
Fat: 6 g (1 g saturated)
Cholesterol: 0 mg
Potassium: 126 mg
Phosphorus: 88 mg
Calcium: 47 mg
Sodium: 613 mg
Iron: 1 mg

SPICY LEMON HUMMUS *p. 24*
(Serving size: ¼ cup)
Calories: 181 kcal
Carbs: 17 g (3 g sugar, 5 g of fiber)
Protein: 6 g
Fat: 11 g (1 g saturated)
Cholesterol: 0 mg
Potassium: 102 mg
Phosphorus: 85 mg
Calcium: 36 mg
Sodium: 144 mg
Iron: 1 mg

SWEET & SPICY BBQ WINGS *p. 32*
Calories: 371 kcal
Carbs: 28 g (27 g sugar, 0 g of fiber)
Protein: 25 g
Fat: 17 g (5 g saturated)
Cholesterol: 144 mg
Potassium: 247 mg
Phosphorus: 153 mg
Calcium: 33 mg
Sodium: 276 mg
Iron: 1 mg

SOUPS

ASIAN SOBA NOODLE SOUP *p. 48*
Calories: 300 kcal
Carbs: 32 g (6 g sugar, 3 g of fiber)
Protein: 24 g
Fat: 8 g (3 g saturated)
Cholesterol: 43 mg
Potassium: 384 mg
Phosphorus: 144 mg
Calcium: 35 mg
Sodium: 1314 mg
Iron: 3 mg

BERRY-PLUM SOUP *p. 47*
Calories: 355 kcal
Carbs: 77 g (51 g sugar, 16 g of fiber)
Protein: 3 g
Fat: 1 g (0 g saturated)
Cholesterol: 0 mg
Potassium: 694 mg
Phosphorus: 89 mg
Calcium: 52 mg
Sodium: 8 mg
Iron: 1 mg

CARROT-GINGER SOUP *p. 42*
Calories: 84 kcal
Carbs: 16 g (8 g sugar, 4 g of fiber)
Protein: 2 g
Fat: 2 g (0 g saturated)
Cholesterol: 0 mg
Potassium: 371 mg
Phosphorus: 49 mg
Calcium: 48 mg
Sodium: 543 mg
Iron: 1 mg

CAULIFLOWER LENTIL SOUP *p. 58*
Calories: 134 kcal
Carbs: 22 g (5 g sugar, 8 g of fiber)
Protein: 8 g
Fat: 2 g (0 g saturated)
Cholesterol: 0 mg
Potassium: 458 mg
Phosphorus: 161 mg
Calcium: 42 mg
Sodium: 506 mg
Iron: 3 mg

CHICKEN SOUP WITH RICE NOODLES *p. 44*
Calories: 242 kcal
Carbs: 32 g (5 g sugar, 5 g of fiber)
Protein: 23 g
Fat: 3 g (1 g saturated)
Cholesterol: 55 mg
Potassium: 509 mg
Phosphorus: 203 mg
Calcium: 66 mg
Sodium: 922 mg
Iron: 1 mg

DAIRY BLUEBERRY SOUP *p. 47*
Calories: 215 kcal
Carbs: 48 g (41 g sugar, 2 g of fiber)
Protein: 4 g
Fat: 2 g (1 g saturated)
Cholesterol: 7 mg
Potassium: 279 mg
Phosphorus: 90 mg
Calcium: 156 mg
Sodium: 51 mg
Iron: 0 mg

GREEN SOUP BOWL *p. 48*
Calories: 185 kcal
Carbs: 21 g (5 g sugar, 9 g of fiber)
Protein: 17 g
Fat: 4 g (1 g saturated)
Cholesterol: 0 mg
Potassium: 794 mg
Phosphorus: 258 mg
Calcium: 79 mg
Sodium: 1340 mg
Iron: 3 mg

MARVELOUS MUSHROOM SOUP *p. 50*
Calories: 76 kcal
Carbs: 9 g (5 g sugar, 2 g of fiber)
Protein: 3 g
Fat: 4 g (1 g saturated)
Cholesterol: 0 mg
Potassium: 519 mg
Phosphorus: 150 mg
Calcium: 14 mg
Sodium: 493 mg
Iron: 1 mg

MOM'S CABBAGE SOUP *p. 40*
Calories: 131 kcal
Carbs: 25 g (10 g sugar, 6 g of fiber)
Protein: 4 g
Fat: 3 g (0 g saturated)
Cholesterol: 0 mg
Potassium: 782 mg
Phosphorus: 104 mg
Calcium: 136 mg
Sodium: 813 mg
Iron: 2 mg

PARSNIP & APPLE SOUP *p. 52*
Calories: 181 kcal
Carbs: 40 g (15 g sugar, 6 g of fiber)
Protein: 3 g
Fat: 2 g (0 g saturated)
Cholesterol: 0 mg
Potassium: 659 mg
Phosphorus: 113 mg
Calcium: 59 mg
Sodium: 496 mg
Iron: 1 mg

STRAWBERRY-RHUBARB SOUP *p. 46*
Calories: 182 kcal
Carbs: 46 g (38 g sugar, 4 g of fiber)
Protein: 2 g
Fat: 1 g (0 g saturated)
Cholesterol: 0 mg
Potassium: 455 mg
Phosphorus: 44 mg
Calcium: 90 mg
Sodium: 5 mg
Iron: 1 mg

SWEET POTATO & SQUASH SOUP *p. 54*
Calories: 174 kcal
Carbs: 39 g (15 g sugar, 5 g of fiber)
Protein: 3 g
Fat: 2 g (0 g saturated)
Cholesterol: 0 mg
Potassium: 869 mg
Phosphorus: 91 mg
Calcium: 101 mg
Sodium: 511 mg
Iron: 2 mg

VEGETABLE SOUP WITH SPAGHETTI SQUASH NOODLES *p. 56*
Calories: 131 kcal
Carbs: 20 g (8 g sugar, 4 g of fiber)
Protein: 3 g
Fat: 3 g (1 g saturated)
Cholesterol: 0 mg
Potassium: 525 mg
Phosphorus: 72 mg
Calcium: 60 mg
Sodium: 629 mg
Iron: 1 mg

WATERMELON FRUIT SOUP *p. 46*
Calories: 94 kcal
Carbs: 24 g (21 g sugar, 1 g of fiber)
Protein: 1 g
Fat: 0 g (0 g saturated)
Cholesterol: 0 mg
Potassium: 240 mg
Phosphorus: 24 mg
Calcium: 17 mg
Sodium: 3 mg
Iron: 1 mg

SALAD

CANDIED NUT SPINACH SALAD *p. 84*
Calories: 306 kcal
Carbs: 26 g (13 g sugar, 6 g of fiber)
Protein: 4 g
Fat: 23 g (3 g saturated)
Cholesterol: 0 mg
Potassium: 362 mg
Phosphorus: 89 mg
Calcium: 40 mg
Sodium: 165 mg
Iron: 2 mg

CRUNCHY CELERY & CUCUMBER SALAD *p. 68*
Calories: 229 kcal
Carbs: 13 g (8 g sugar, 3 g of fiber)
Protein: 3 g
Fat: 19 g (3 g saturated)
Cholesterol: 0 mg
Potassium: 474 mg
Phosphorus: 21 mg
Calcium: 79 mg
Sodium: 754 mg
Iron: 1 mg

EDAMAME, CORN & BLACK BEAN SALAD *p. 62*
Calories: 223 kcal
Carbs: 23 g (7 g sugar, 3 g of fiber)
Protein: 7 g
Fat: 12 g (1 g saturated)
Cholesterol: 0 mg
Potassium: 225 mg
Phosphorus: 71 mg
Calcium: 28 mg
Sodium: 377 mg
Iron: 1 mg

EXOTIC ISLAND SALAD *p. 74*
Calories: 214 kcal
Carbs: 23 g (7 g sugar, 7 g of fiber)
Protein: 4 g
Fat: 13 g (2 g saturated)
Cholesterol: 0 mg
Potassium: 467 mg
Phosphorus: 57 mg
Calcium: 44 mg
Sodium: 324 mg
Iron: 1 mg

FENNEL & RADISH SALAD *p. 72*
Calories: 148 kcal
Carbs: 16 g (12 g sugar, 3 g of fiber)
Protein: 1 g
Fat: 9 g (1 g saturated)
Cholesterol: 0 g
Potassium: 264 mg
Phosphorus: 33 mg
Calcium: 33 mg
Sodium: 273mg
Iron: 0 mg

FRESH MANGO SALAD *p. 78*
Calories: 270 kcal
Carbs: 47 g (41 g sugar, 5 g of fiber)
Protein: 3 g
Fat: 11 g (2 g saturated)
Cholesterol: 0 mg
Potassium: 534 mg
Phosphorus: 47 mg
Calcium: 45 mg
Sodium: 167 mg
Iron: 1 mg

GREEN SALAD WITH MUSHROOMS & QUINOA *p. 80*
Calories: 266 kcal
Carbs: 22 g (5 g sugar, 5g of fiber)
Protein: 5 g
Fat: 18 g (3 g saturated)
Cholesterol: 0 mg
Potassium: 411 mg
Phosphorus: 129 mg
Calcium: 63 mg
Sodium: 204 mg
Iron: 2 mg

HAWAIIAN COLESLAW *p. 88*
Calories: 168 kcal
Carbs: 20 g (14 g sugar, 4 g of fiber)
Protein: 2 g
Fat: 10 g (1 g saturated)
Cholesterol: 0 mg
Potassium: 254 mg
Phosphorus: 30 mg
Calcium: 58 mg
Sodium: 512 mg
Iron: 1 mg

KALE SALAD WITH ROASTED SWEET POTATOES *p. 90*
Calories: 218 kcal
Carbs: 33 g (22 g sugar, 4g of fiber)
Protein: 3 g
Fat: 9 g (1 g saturated)
Cholesterol: 0 mg
Potassium: 422 mg
Phosphorus: 62 mg
Calcium: 79 mg
Sodium: 381 mg
Iron: 1 mg

LENTIL CRANBERRY SALAD *p. 76*
Calories: 302 kcal
Carbs: 37 g (13 g sugar, 14 g of fiber)
Protein: 11 g
Fat: 13 g (2 g saturated)
Cholesterol: 0 mg
Potassium: 40 mg
Phosphorus: 7 mg
Calcium: 32 mg
Sodium: 528 mg
Iron: 4 mg

RED CABBAGE & KALE SALAD *p. 66*
Calories: 189 kcal
Carbs: 18 g (8 g sugar, 5 g of fiber)
Protein: 8 g
Fat: 12 g (2 saturated)
Cholesterol: 0 mg
Potassium: 608 mg
Phosphorus: 196 mg
Calcium: 155 mg
Sodium: 720mg
Iron: 4 mg

ROASTED BEET SALAD WITH LEMON-BASIL DRESSING *p. 64*
Calories: 126 kcal
Carbs: 12 g (9 g sugar, 2 g of fiber)
Protein: 2 g
Fat: 8 g (1 g saturated)
Cholesterol: 0 mg
Potassium: 203 mg
Phosphorus: 35 mg
Calcium: 35 mg
Sodium: 177 mg
Iron: 1 mg

SHAVED CORN & ASPARAGUS SALAD p. 70
Calories: 199 kcal
Carbs: 25 g (6 g sugar, 4 g of fiber)
Protein: 5 g
Fat: 11 g (2 g saturated)
Cholesterol: 0 mg
Potassium: 373 mg
Phosphorus: 108 mg
Calcium: 19 mg
Sodium: 248 mg
Iron: 1 mg

SNAP PEA SALAD WITH BASIL-MINT DRESSING p. 82
Calories: 158 kcal
Carbs: 18 g (13 g sugar, 2 g of fiber)
Protein: 2 g
Fat: 9 g (1 g saturated)
Cholesterol: 0 mg
Potassium: 87 mg
Phosphorus: 19 mg
Calcium: 59 mg
Sodium: 160 mg
Iron: 1 mg

TOMATO DILL SALAD p. 86
Calories: 111 kcal
Carbs: 6 g (3 g sugar, 2 g of fiber)
Protein: 1 g
Fat: 10 g (1 g saturated)
Cholesterol: 0 mg
Potassium: 310 mg
Phosphorus: 32 mg
Calcium: 21 mg
Sodium: 158 mg
Iron: 1 mg

FISH

BAKED FISH FILLETS & SAUTÉED MUSHROOMS p. 110
Calories: 199 kcal
Carbs: 5 g (2 g sugar, 1 g of fiber)
Protein: 20 g
Fat: 10 g (1 g saturated)
Cholesterol: 71 mg
Potassium: 423 mg
Phosphorus: 432 mg
Calcium: 42 mg
Sodium: 783 mg
Iron: 1 mg

BALSAMIC HONEY-GLAZED SALMON p. 94
Calories: 342 kcal
Carbs: 17 g (15 g sugar, 0 g of fiber)
Protein: 39 g
Fat: 12 g (2 g saturated)
Cholesterol: 107 mg
Potassium: 984 mg
Phosphorus: 395 mg
Calcium: 32 mg
Sodium: 179 mg
Iron: 2 mg

BROILED LEMON FISH FILLETS p. 106
Calories: 158 kcal
Carbs: 1 g (0 g sugar, 0 g of fiber)
Protein: 24 g
Fat: 6 g (1 g saturated)
Cholesterol: 88 mg
Potassium: 316 mg
Phosphorus: 484 mg
Calcium: 44 mg
Sodium: 568 mg
Iron: 1 mg

CEDAR-PLANKED SALMON WITH STRAWBERRY-CHILI SALSA p. 96
Calories: 374 kcal
Carbs: 9 g (5 g sugar, 2 g of fiber)
Protein: 39 g
Fat: 20 g (3 g saturated)
Cholesterol: 107 mg
Potassium: 1117 mg
Phosphorus: 414 mg
Calcium: 43 mg
Sodium: 567 mg
Iron: 2 mg

HALIBUT FISH STICKS p. 100
Calories: 510 kcal
Carbs: 24 g (3 g sugar, 1 g of fiber)
Protein: 32 g
Fat: 32 g (6 g saturated)
Cholesterol: 178 mg
Potassium: 573 mg
Phosphorus: 372 mg
Calcium: 21 mg
Sodium: 383 mg
Iron: 10 mg

HALIBUT, GRAPEFRUIT & SPINACH SALAD p. 102
(Nutrient values for main dish serving appear in **bold***; for appetizer servings in* regular*)*
Calories: **684 kcal** (342 kcal)
Carbs: **19 g (4 g sugar, 2 g of fiber)** (9 g [2 g sugar, 1 g fiber])
Protein: **36 g** (18 g protein)
Fat: **51 g (8 g saturated)** (26 g [4 g saturated])
Cholesterol: **112 mg** (56 mg)
Potassium: **839 mg** (419 mg)
Phosphorus: **415 mg** (208 mg)
Calcium: **39 mg** (19 mg)
Sodium: **236 mg** (118 mg)
Iron: **3 mg** (1 mg)

HERBED SALMON p. 98
Calories: 318 kcal
Carbs: 8 g (4 g sugar, 1 g of fiber)
Protein: 35 g
Fat: 16 g (2 g saturated)
Cholesterol: 96 mg
Potassium: 1038 mg
Phosphorus: 368 mg
Calcium: 72 mg
Sodium: 90 mg
Iron: 3 mg

LEMON-SPINACH PESTO FILLETS p. 108
Calories: 640 kcal
Carbs: 3 g (1 g sugar, 1 g of fiber)
Protein: 34 g
Fat: 54 g (9 g saturated)
Cholesterol: 105 mg
Potassium: 759 mg
Phosphorus: 411 mg
Calcium: 96 mg
Sodium: 751 mg
Iron: 2 mg

MAPLE-GLAZED SALMON p. 95
Calories: 341 kcal
Carbs: 15 g (14 g sugar, 0 g of fiber)
Protein: 40 g
Fat: 12 g (2 g saturated)
Cholesterol: 107 mg
Potassium: 1011 mg
Phosphorus: 393 mg
Calcium: 49 mg
Sodium: 776 mg
Iron: 2 mg

SEA BASS WITH LEMON BUTTER SAUCE p. 104
Calories: 339 kcal
Carbs: 2 g (1 g sugar, 0 g of fiber)
Protein: 33 g
Fat: 21 g (11 g saturated)
Cholesterol: 115 mg
Potassium: 507 mg
Phosphorus: 358 mg
Calcium: 29 mg
Sodium: 125 mg
Iron: 1 mg

STICKY SESAME SALMON p. 94
Calories: 405 kcal
Carbs: 26 g (23 g sugar, 1 g of fiber)
Protein: 41 g
Fat: 15 g (2 g saturated)
Cholesterol: 107 mg
Potassium: 1019 mg
Phosphorus: 432 mg
Calcium: 90 mg
Sodium: 548 mg
Iron: 3 mg

TILAPIA & RICE WITH SUNNY-SIDE-UP EGGS p. 112
Calories: 526 kcal
Carbs: 58 g (2 g sugar, 2 g of fiber)
Protein: 41 g
Fat: 15 g (3 g saturated)
Cholesterol: 220 mg
Potassium: 651 mg
Phosphorus: 340 mg
Calcium: 72 mg
Sodium: 121 mg
Iron: 3 mg

POULTRY

BASIL-MARINATED CHICKEN *p. 121*
Calories: 191 kcal
Carbs: 1 g (0 g sugar, 0 g of fiber)
Protein: 27 g
Fat: 8 g (2 g saturated)
Cholesterol: 73 mg
Potassium: 250 mg
Phosphorus: 203 mg
Calcium: 22 mg
Sodium: 66 mg
Iron: 1 mg

BASIL CHICKEN
WITH SUN-DRIED TOMATOES *p. 134*
Calories: 528 kcal
Carbs: 15 g (8 g sugar, 2 g of fiber)
Protein: 43 g
Fat: 31 g (7 g saturated)
Cholesterol: 132 mg
Potassium: 374 mg
Phosphorus: 281 mg
Calcium: 45 mg
Sodium: 163 mg
Iron: 3 mg

BEER-MARINATED CHICKEN *p. 120*
Calories: 215 kcal
Carbs: 1 g (0 g sugar, 0 g of fiber)
Protein: 27 g
Fat: 10 g (2 g saturated)
Cholesterol: 73 mg
Potassium: 235 mg
Phosphorus: 199 mg
Calcium: 22 mg
Sodium: 65 mg
Iron: 1 mg

CANDIED CURRY CHICKEN *p. 138*
Calories: 505 kcal
Carbs: 32 g (13 g sugar, 1 g of fiber)
Protein: 44 g
Fat: 22 g (6 g saturated)
Cholesterol: 178 mg
Potassium: 405 mg
Phosphorus: 302 mg
Calcium: 43 mg
Sodium: 782 mg
Iron: 8 mg

CHICKEN, MANGO &
AVOCADO SALAD *p. 122*
Calories: 473 kcal
Carbs: 25 g (16 g sugar, 7 g of fiber)
Protein: 21 g
Fat: 33 g (5 g saturated)
Cholesterol: 49 mg
Potassium: 689 mg
Phosphorus: 186 mg
Calcium: 61 mg
Sodium: 232 mg
Iron: 2 mg

CHINESE CHICKEN & MUSHROOMS *p. 128*
Calories: 263 kcal
Carbs: 18 g (11 g sugar, 2 g of fiber)
Protein: 30 g
Fat: 8 g (1 g saturated)
Cholesterol: 73 mg
Potassium: 434 mg
Phosphorus: 243 mg
Calcium: 33 mg
Sodium: 687 mg
Iron: 2 mg

GRILLED CHICKEN WITH
CARAMELIZED ONIONS *p. 118*
Calories: 237 kcal
Carbs: 8 g (3 g sugar, 1 g of fiber)
Protein: 28 g
Fat: 10 g (2 g saturated)
Cholesterol: 73 mg
Potassium: 337 mg
Phosphorus: 220 mg
Calcium: 34 mg
Sodium: 67 mg
Iron: 1 mg

HONEY-ROASTED CHICKEN
WITH SQUASH & ONIONS *p. 132*
Calories: 568 kcal
Carbs: 55 g (40 g sugar, 5 g of fiber)
Protein: 43 g
Fat: 21 g (6 g saturated)
Cholesterol: 131 mg
Potassium: 833 mg
Phosphorus: 334 mg
Calcium: 99 mg
Sodium: 140 mg
Iron: 3 mg

LEMON-HERB CHICKEN WITH
ROASTED GARLIC *p. 136*
Calories: 534 kcal
Carbs: 13 g (9 g sugar, 1 g of fiber)
Protein: 42 g
Fat: 35 g (8 g saturated)
Cholesterol: 132 mg
Potassium: 419 mg
Phosphorus: 291 mg
Calcium: 50 mg
Sodium: 127 mg
Iron: 2 mg

MANGO CHICKEN
WITH LEEKS & RED PEPPERS *p. 130*
Calories: 502 kcal
Carbs: 29 g (23 g sugar, 3 g of fiber)
Protein: 43 g
Fat: 24g (6 g saturated)
Cholesterol: 132 mg
Potassium: 613 mg
Phosphorus: 306 mg
Calcium: 58 mg
Sodium: 251 mg
Iron: 3 mg

ORANGE & SOY-MARINATED CHICKEN
p. 120
Calories: 253 kcal
Carbs: 2 g (1 g sugar, 0 g of fiber)
Protein: 28 g
Fat: 14 g (2 g saturated)
Cholesterol: 73 mg
Potassium: 253 mg
Phosphorus: 199 mg
Calcium: 21 mg
Sodium: 677 mg
Iron: 1 mg

RICE NOODLE STIR-FRY/PANCIT *p. 126*
Calories: 332 kcal
Carbs: 32 g (5 g sugar, 5 g of fiber)
Protein: 33 g
Fat: 8 g (1 g saturated)
Cholesterol: 73 mg
Potassium: 420 mg
Phosphorus: 223 mg
Calcium: 60 mg
Sodium: 1081 mg
Iron: 2 mg

ROLLED TURKEY ROAST
WITH DELI STRIPS *p. 142*
Calories: 297 kcal
Carbs: 20 g (19 g sugar, 0 g of fiber)
Protein: 31 g
Fat: 10 g (3 g saturated)
Cholesterol: 103 mg
Potassium: 273 mg
Phosphorus: 230 mg
Calcium: 26 mg
Sodium: 824 mg
Iron: 2 mg

SESAME-GINGER CHICKEN *p. 140*
Calories: 468 kcal
Carbs: 20 g (17 g sugar, 1 g of fiber)
Protein: 44 g
Fat: 23 g (6 g saturated)
Cholesterol: 132 mg
Potassium: 397 mg
Phosphorus: 307 mg
Calcium: 84 mg
Sodium: 1238 mg
Iron: 3 mg

SWEET & SOUR CHINESE CHICKEN *p. 116*
Calories: 356 kcal
Carbs: 37 g (17 g sugar, 0 g of fiber)
Protein: 30 g
Fat: 9 g (2 g saturated)
Cholesterol: 135 mg
Potassium: 249 mg
Phosphorus: 228 mg
Calcium: 23 mg
Sodium: 650 mg
Iron: 1 mg

TERIYAKI CHICKEN *p. 121*

Calories: 280 kcal
Carbs: 13 g (12 g sugar, 0 g of fiber)
Protein: 28 g
Fat: 12 g (2 g saturated)
Cholesterol: 73 mg
Potassium: 244 mg
Phosphorus: 200 mg
Calcium: 18 mg
Sodium: 678 mg
Iron: 1 mg

THREE-SEEDED SCHNITZEL *p. 124*

Calories: 378 kcal
Carbs: 19 g (1 g sugar, 3 g of fiber)
Protein: 37 g
Fat: 17 g (3 g saturated)
Cholesterol: 146 mg
Potassium: 352 mg
Phosphorus: 341 mg
Calcium: 145 mg
Sodium: 128 mg
Iron: 3 mg

MEAT

BALSAMIC-BRAISED BRISKET *p. 160*

Calories: 673 kcal
Carbs: 19 g (12 g sugar, 3 g of fiber)
Protein: 44 g
Fat: 44 g (16 g saturated)
Cholesterol: 152 mg
Potassium: 786 mg
Phosphorus: 373 mg
Calcium: 40 mg
Sodium: 662 mg
Iron: 5 mg

BEEF STIR-FRY WITH KALE & PEPPERS *p. 168*

Calories: 489 kcal
Carbs: 17 g (6 g sugar, 3 g of fiber)
Protein: 38 g
Fat: 30 g (9 g saturated)
Cholesterol: 101 mg
Potassium: 855 mg
Phosphorus: 321 mg
Calcium: 99 mg
Sodium: 1320 mg
Iron: 5 mg

BEST ROAST BRISKET *p. 162*

Calories: 855 kcal
Carbs: 25 g (19 g sugar, 2 g of fiber)
Protein: 61 g
Fat: 56 g (21 g saturated)
Cholesterol: 211 mg
Potassium: 733 mg
Phosphorus: 499 mg
Calcium: 53 mg
Sodium: 1166 mg
Iron: 6 mg

BOURBON MARINATED PRIME RIB *p. 158*

Calories: 502 kcal
Carbs: 12 g (12 g sugar, 0 g of fiber)
Protein: 64 g
Fat: 16 g (6 g saturated)
Cholesterol: 188 mg
Potassium: 898 mg
Phosphorus: 568 mg
Calcium: 18 mg
Sodium: 736 mg
Iron: 6 mg

CHUNKY CHILI *p. 174*

Calories: 460 kcal
Carbs: 53 g (7 g sugar, 18 g of fiber)
Protein: 32 g
Fat: 15 g (4 g saturated)
Cholesterol: 48 mg
Potassium: 1156 mg
Phosphorus: 401 mg
Calcium: 197 mg
Sodium: 1353 mg
Iron: 7 mg

COFFEE-RUBBED LONDON BROIL *p. 150*

Calories: 318 kcal
Carbs: 9 g (6 g sugar, 1 g of fiber)
Protein: 39 g
Fat: 13 g (5 g saturated)
Cholesterol: 115 mg
Potassium: 354 mg
Phosphorus: 241 mg
Calcium: 16 mg
Sodium: 414 mg
Iron: 4 mg

CRANBERRY-GLAZED CORNED BEEF *p. 164*

Calories: 627 kcal
Carbs: 18 g (15 g sugar, 0 g of fiber)
Protein: 43 g
Fat: 40 g (15 g saturated)
Cholesterol: 152 mg
Potassium: 416 mg
Phosphorus: 341 mg
Calcium: 13 mg
Sodium: 572 mg
Iron: 4 mg

JALAPEÑO SHORT RIBS *p. 152*

Calories: 457 kcal
Carbs: 27 g (23 g sugar, 3 g of fiber)
Protein: 38 g
Fat: 22 g (9 g saturated)
Cholesterol: 109 mg
Potassium: 772 mg
Phosphorus: 315 mg
Calcium: 55 mg
Sodium: 1145 mg
Iron: 6 mg

LEMON-LIME LAMB CHOPS *p. 170*

Calories: 247 kcal
Carbs: 5 g (1 g sugar, 1 g of fiber)
Protein: 28 g
Fat: 13 g (4 g saturated)
Cholesterol: 87 mg
Potassium: 417 mg
Phosphorus: 219 mg
Calcium: 32 mg
Sodium: 78 mg
Iron: 2 mg

MAPLE-MUSTARD MIAMI RIBS *p. 156*

Calories: 445 kcal
Carbs: 33 g (29 g sugar, 1 g of fiber)
Protein: 15 g
Fat: 28 g (12 g saturated)
Cholesterol: 62 mg
Potassium: 291 mg
Phosphorus: 118 mg
Calcium: 58 mg
Sodium: 400 mg
Iron: 2 mg

MARINATED SKIRT STEAK *p. 146*

Calories: 479 kcal
Carbs: 13 g (11 g sugar, 0 g of fiber)
Protein: 52 g
Fat: 24 g (9 g saturated)
Cholesterol: 157 mg
Potassium: 549 mg
Phosphorus: 294 mg
Calcium: 22 mg
Sodium: 1032 mg
Iron: 4 mg

QUICK SKILLET DINNER *p. 176*

Calories: 451 kcal
Carbs: 38 g (7 g sugar, 4 g of fiber)
Protein: 33 g
Fat: 19 g (7 g saturated)
Cholesterol: 95 mg
Potassium: 893 mg
Phosphorus: 327 mg
Calcium: 99 mg
Sodium: 920 mg
Iron: 6 mg

RASPBERRY LONDON BROIL *p. 148*

Calories: 368 kcal
Carbs: 33 g (29 g sugar, 0 g of fiber)
Protein: 33 g
Fat: 11 g (4 g saturated)
Cholesterol: 96 mg
Potassium: 264 mg
Phosphorus: 197 mg
Calcium: 12 mg
Sodium: 629 mg
Iron: 3 mg

STICKY MIAMI RIBS *p. 154*
Calories: 270 kcal
Carbs: 14 g (13 g sugar, 0 g of fiber)
Protein: 11 g
Fat: 18 g (8 g saturated)
Cholesterol: 41 mg
Potassium: 139 mg
Phosphorus: 77 mg
Calcium: 11 mg
Sodium: 1009 mg
Iron: 1 mg

STUFFED EGGPLANT *p. 172*
Calories: 479 kcal
Carbs: 27 g (7 g sugar, 7 g of fiber)
Protein: 22 g
Fat: 34 g (7 g saturated)
Cholesterol: 48 mg
Potassium: 657 mg
Phosphorus: 401 mg
Calcium: 88 mg
Sodium: 226 mg
Iron: 4 mg

SWEET & TANGY PICKLED TONGUE *p. 166*
Calories: 723 kcal
Carbs: 21 g (21 g sugar, 0 g of fiber)
Protein: 44 g
Fat: 51 g (18 g saturated)
Cholesterol: 299 mg
Potassium: 442 mg
Phosphorus: 330 mg
Calcium: 27 mg
Sodium: 299 mg
Iron: 6 mg

DAIRY

CAPRESE PENNE SALAD *p. 190*
Calories: 414 kcal
Carbs: 58 g (4 g sugar, 2 g of fiber)
Protein: 21 g
Fat: 10 g (5 g saturated)
Cholesterol: 23 mg
Potassium: 168 mg
Phosphorus: 232 mg
Calcium: 316 mg
Sodium: 274 mg
Iron: 1 mg

CAULIFLOWER-CRUSTED PIZZA *p. 198*
Calories: 299 kcal
Carbs: 11 g (5 g sugar, 4 g of fiber)
Protein: 25 g
Fat: 18 g (9 g saturated)
Cholesterol: 89 mg
Potassium: 443 mg
Phosphorus: 486 mg
Calcium: 612 mg
Sodium: 1296 mg
Iron: 1 mg

CHEESY QUINOA BITES *p. 180*
(Serving size: 2 muffins; approx. 50 g)
Calories: 93 kcal
Carbs: 11 g (1 g sugar, 1 g of fiber)
Protein: 5 g
Fat: 3 g (1 g saturated)
Cholesterol: 35 mg
Potassium: 140 mg
Phosphorus: 122 mg
Calcium: 70 mg
Sodium: 173 mg
Iron: 1 mg

CHEESY SMASHED ROASTED POTATOES *p. 184*
Calories: 264 kcal
Carbs: 26 g (1g sugar, 2 g of fiber)
Protein: 12 g
Fat: 12 g (5 g saturated)
Cholesterol: 20 mg
Potassium: 446 mg
Phosphorus: 248 mg
Calcium: 286 mg
Sodium: 253 mg
Iron: 0 mg

CRUSTLESS SPINACH & FETA CHEESE TART *p. 188*
Calories: 164 kcal
Carbs: 13 g (2 g sugar, 4 g of fiber)
Protein: 10 g
Fat: 9 g (5 g saturated)
Cholesterol: 147 mg
Potassium: 99 mg
Phosphorus: 151 mg
Calcium: 207 mg
Sodium: 404 mg
Iron: 3 mg

DOUBLE CHEESE CAULIFLOWER GRATIN *p. 186*
Calories: 374 kcal
Carbs: 22 g (4 g sugar, 4 g of fiber)
Protein: 22 g
Fat: 22 g (14 g saturated)
Cholesterol: 68 mg
Potassium: 266 mg
Phosphorus: 407 mg
Calcium: 541 mg
Sodium: 557 mg
Iron: 1 mg

FRESH BERRY TOAST *p. 194*
Calories: 379 kcal
Carbs: 50 g (18 g sugar, 4 g of fiber)
Protein: 20 g
Fat: 12 g (6 g saturated)
Cholesterol: 38 mg
Potassium: 425 mg
Phosphorus: 311 mg
Calcium: 490 mg
Sodium: 370 mg
Iron: 3mg

GOURMET GARLICKY CHEESY BREAD *p. 182*
Calories: 152 kcal
Carbs: 4 g (0 g sugar, 0 g of fiber)
Protein: 8 g
Fat: 12 g (7 g saturated)
Cholesterol: 31 mg
Potassium: 51 mg
Phosphorus: 154 mg
Calcium: 215 mg
Sodium: 197 mg
Iron: 0 mg

GRANDMA MARION'S CHEESE MUFFINS *p. 200*
(Serving size: 1 muffin)
Calories: 156 kcal
Carbs: 14 g (5 g sugar, 0 g of fiber)
Protein: 6 g
Fat: 9 g (5 g saturated)
Cholesterol: 58 mg
Potassium: 29 mg
Phosphorus: 46mg
Calcium: 73 mg
Sodium: 185 mg
Iron: 1 mg

LEMON GARLIC SPAGHETTI *p. 196*
Calories: 584 kcal
Carbs: 74 g (2 g sugar, 4 g of fiber)
Protein: 17 g
Fat: 24 g (5 g saturated)
Cholesterol: 9 mg
Potassium: 170 mg
Phosphorus: 203 mg
Calcium: 142 mg
Sodium: 656 mg
Iron: 3 mg

ROASTED BALSAMIC TOMATOES & FETA CHEESE *p. 192*
Calories: 207 kcal
Carbs: 11 g (8 g sugar, 3 g of fiber)
Protein: 7 g
Fat: 15 g (7 g saturated)
Cholesterol: 33 mg
Potassium: 525 mg
Phosphorus: 178 mg
Calcium: 209 mg
Sodium: 836 mg
Iron: 1 mg

GRAIN SIDE DISHES

APPLE-CRANBERRY COUSCOUS *p. 204*
Calories: 535 kcal
Carbs: 92 g (35 g sugar, 7 g of fiber)
Protein: 8 g
Fat: 15 g (2 g saturated)
Cholesterol: 0 mg
Potassium: 185 mg
Phosphorus: 120 mg
Calcium: 19 mg
Sodium: 487 mg
Iron: 1 mg

BLACK RICE WITH MANGO, POMEGRANATE & AVOCADO p. 210

Calories: 458 kcal
Carbs: 70 g (27 g sugar, 9 g fiber)
Protein: 7 g
Fat: 20 g (3 g saturated)
Cholesterol: 0 mg
Potassium: 468 mg
Phosphorus: 47 mg
Calcium: 36 mg
Sodium: 51 mg
Iron: 2 mg

CURRIED BASMATI PILAF p. 208

Calories: 524 kcal
Carbs: 108 g (23 g sugar, 6 g fiber)
Protein: 7 g
Fat: 7 g (1 g saturated)
Cholesterol: 0 mg
Potassium: 100 mg
Phosphorus: 23 mg
Calcium: 61 mg
Sodium: 2 mg
Iron: 1 mg

LEMON-INFUSED LENTIL RICE p. 206

Calories: 337 kcal
Carbs: 53 g (5 g sugar, 11 g of fiber)
Protein: 13 g
Fat: 9 g (1 g saturated)
Cholesterol: 0 mg
Potassium: 423 mg
Phosphorus: 192 mg
Calcium: 69 mg
Sodium: 870 mg
Iron: 4 mg

QUINOA WITH DRIED FRUIT & RED CABBAGE p. 218

Calories: 327 kcal
Carbs: 49 g (26 g sugar, 5 g fiber)
Protein: 6 g
Fat: 13 g (2 g saturated)
Cholesterol: 0 mg
Potassium: 442 mg
Phosphorus: 167 mg
Calcium: 38 mg
Sodium: 354 mg
Iron: 2 mg

QUINOA WITH HEARTS OF PALM, CHERRY TOMATOES & AVOCADO p. 214

Calories: 327 kcal
Carbs: 49 g (26 g sugar, 5 g fiber)
Protein: 6 g
Fat: 13 g (2 g saturated)
Cholesterol: 0 mg
Potassium: 442 mg
Phosphorus: 167 mg
Calcium: 38 mg
Sodium: 354 mg
Iron: 2 mg

QUINOA WITH NECTARINES & PICKLED ONIONS p. 216

Calories: 215 kcal
Carbs: 34 g (9 g sugar, 3 g fiber)
Protein: 5 g
Fat: 7 g (1 g saturated)
Cholesterol: 0 mg
Potassium: 275 mg
Phosphorus: 159 mg
Calcium: 24 mg
Sodium: 732 mg
Iron: 2 mg

QUINOA WITH ROASTED VEGGIES p. 220

Calories: 222 kcal
Carbs: 24 g (5 g sugar, 3 g fiber)
Protein: 5 g
Fat: 12 g (2 g saturated)
Cholesterol: 0 mg
Potassium: 326 mg
Phosphorus: 142 mg
Calcium: 30 mg
Sodium: 299 mg
Iron: 2 mg

RICE NOODLES WITH CRUNCHY VEGGIES p. 222

Calories: 254 kcal
Carbs: 24 g (2 g sugar, 4 g fiber)
Protein: 7 g
Fat: 15 g (2 g saturated)
Cholesterol: 0 mg
Potassium: 211 mg
Phosphorus: 164 mg
Calcium: 70 mg
Sodium: 597 mg
Iron: 2 mg

WHEAT BERRIES WITH KALE & MANGO p. 224

Calories: 292 kcal
Carbs: 47 g (19 g sugar, 8 g fiber)
Protein: 6 g
Fat: 11 g (1 g saturated)
Cholesterol: 0 mg
Potassium: 407 mg
Phosphorus: 46 mg
Calcium: 75 mg
Sodium: 14 mg
Iron: 2 mg

WILD RICE WITH ROASTED PEPPERS & CANDIED ALMONDS p. 212

Calories: 264 kcal
Carbs: 44 g (15 g sugar, 4 g fiber)
Protein: 7 g
Fat: 7 g (1 g saturated)
Cholesterol: 0 mg
Potassium: 297 mg
Phosphorus: 147 mg
Calcium: 35 mg
Sodium: 248 mg
Iron: 1 mg

VEGETABLE SIDE DISHES

ASPARAGUS & MUSHROOM STIR-FRY p. 230

Calories: 101 kcal
Carbs: 13 g (4 g sugar, 4 g of fiber)
Protein: 5 g
Fat: 5 g (1 g saturated)
Cholesterol: 0 mg
Potassium: 473 mg
Phosphorus: 136 mg
Calcium: 52 mg
Sodium: 20 mg
Iron: 2 mg

CRUNCHY GINGERED GREEN BEANS p. 232

Calories: 114 kcal
Carbs: 13 g (2 g sugar, 5 g of fiber)
Protein: 4 g
Fat: 6 g (1 g saturated)
Cholesterol: 0 mg
Potassium: 237 mg
Phosphorus: 64 mg
Calcium: 96 mg
Sodium: 309 mg
Iron: 1 mg

GREAT BUB'S OVERNIGHT POTATONIK p. 246

Calories: 267 kcal
Carbs: 48 g (3 g sugar, 4 g of fiber)
Protein: 6 g
Fat: 6 g (1 g saturated)
Cholesterol: 56 mg
Potassium: 805 mg
Phosphorus: 125 mg
Calcium: 31 mg
Sodium: 1183 mg
Iron: 1 mg

HERB-ROASTED DIJON ONIONS p. 240

Calories: 218 kcal
Carbs: 29 g (16 g sugar, 3 g of fiber)
Protein: 3 g
Fat: 11 g (2 g saturated)
Cholesterol: 0 mg
Potassium: 387 mg
Phosphorus: 72 mg
Calcium: 62 mg
Sodium: 192 mg
Iron: 1 mg

MAPLE-DIJON CABBAGE ROUNDS p. 236

Calories: 156 kcal
Carbs: 18 g (13 g sugar, 3 g of fiber)
Protein: 2 g
Fat: 9 g (1 g saturated)
Cholesterol: 0 mg
Potassium: 317 mg
Phosphorus: 50 mg
Calcium: 85 mg
Sodium: 73 mg
Iron: 0 mg

PANKO-TOPPED BOK CHOY & EDAMAME p. 234

Calories: 275 kcal

Carbs: 36 g (13 g sugar, 15 g of fiber)

Protein: 18 g

Fat: 10 g (1 g saturated)

Cholesterol: 0 mg

Potassium: 279 mg

Phosphorus: 93 mg

Calcium: 961 mg

Sodium: 816 mg

Iron: 10 mg

PARSNIP POTATO LATKES p. 242
(serving size: 1 latke, including sour cream)

Calories: 139 kcal

Carbs: 17 g (4 g sugar, 2 g of fiber)

Protein: 3 g

Fat: 6 g (4 g saturated)

Cholesterol: 51 mg

Potassium: 259 mg

Phosphorus: 67 mg

Calcium: 66 mg

Sodium: 227 mg

Iron: 1 mg

RAINBOW ROASTED ROOTS WITH ORANGES & POMEGRANATES p. 250

Calories: 198 kcal

Carbs: 32 g (18 g sugar, 5 g of fiber)

Protein: 3 g

Fat: 7 g (1 g saturated)

Cholesterol: 0 mg

Potassium: 605 mg

Phosphorus: 84 mg

Calcium: 60 mg

Sodium: 51 mg

Iron: 1 mg

ROASTED ASPARAGUS & GARLIC p. 228

Calories: 115 kcal

Carbs: 11 g (2 g sugar, 3 g of fiber)

Protein: 4 g

Fat: 7 g (1 g saturated)

Cholesterol: 0 mg

Potassium: 388 mg

Phosphorus: 97 mg

Calcium: 60 mg

Sodium: 23 mg

Iron: 2 mg

ROASTED BABY POTATO & TOMATO MEDLEY p. 244

Calories: 183 kcal

Carbs: 33 g (2 g sugar, 3 g of fiber)

Protein: 3 g

Fat: 5 g (1 g saturated)

Cholesterol: 0 mg

Potassium: 626 mg

Phosphorus: 78 mg

Calcium: 22 mg

Sodium: 15 mg

Iron: 1 mg

ROASTED SQUASH WITH RED ONION & PEARS p. 252

Calories: 181 kcal

Carbs: 36 g (22 g sugar, 7 g of fiber)

Protein: 2 g

Fat: 4 g (1 g saturated)

Cholesterol: 0 mg

Potassium: 430 mg

Phosphorus: 43 mg

Calcium: 43 mg

Sodium: 5 mg

Iron: 1 mg

SPICED CAULIFLOWER p. 238

Calories: 94 kcal

Carbs: 11 g (7 g sugar, 3 g of fiber)

Protein: 3 g

Fat: 5 g (1 g saturated)

Cholesterol: 0 mg

Potassium: 217 mg

Phosphorus: 47 mg

Calcium: 28 mg

Sodium: 502 mg

Iron: 1 mg

SWEET POTATO SCALLOP p. 248

Calories: 263 kcal

Carbs: 45 g (23 g sugar, 6 g of fiber)

Protein: 4 g

Fat: 8 g (1 g saturated)

Cholesterol: 0 mg

Potassium: 828 mg

Phosphorus: 107 mg

Calcium: 94 mg

Sodium: 62 mg

Iron: 2 mg

ZUCCHINI-SPINACH KUGELS p. 254
Nutrients per kugel

Calories: 174 kcal

Carbs: 16 g (7 g sugar, 1 g fiber)

Protein: 3 g

Fat: 11 g (1 g saturated)

Cholesterol: 34 mg

Potassium: 81 mg

Phosphorus: 45 mg

Calcium: 38 mg

Sodium: 115 mg

Iron: 1 mg

COOKIES, SQUARES, & TREATS

1-2-3 ALMOND COOKIES p. 258
(Serving size: 1 cookie)

Calories: 64 kcal

Carbs: 5 g (3 g sugar, 1 g of fiber)

Protein: 2 g

Fat: 4 g (0 g saturated)

Cholesterol: 0 mg

Potassium: 68 mg

Phosphorus: 43 mg

Calcium: 24 mg

Sodium: 2 mg

Iron: 0 mg

CANDIED CINNAMON NUTS p. 280
(Serving size: ¼ cup)

Calories: 222 kcal

Carbs: 23 g (18 g sugar, 4 g of fiber)

Protein: 6 g

Fat: 13 g (1 g saturated)

Cholesterol: 0 mg

Potassium: 200 mg

Phosphorus: 130 mg

Calcium: 77 mg

Sodium: 0 mg

Iron: 1 mg

CHEWY RASPBERRY-OATMEAL BARS p. 274
(Serving size: 1 bar)

Calories: 146 kcal

Carbs: 21 g (12 g sugar, 1 g of fiber)

Protein: 2 g

Fat: 7 g (1 g saturated)

Cholesterol: 5 mg

Potassium: 18 mg

Phosphorus: 16 mg

Calcium: 24 mg

Sodium: 31 mg

Iron: 1 mg

CHOCOLATE-DIPPED CHIPS p. 282

Calories: 208 kcal

Carbs: 27 g (23 g sugar, 2 g of fiber)

Protein: 2 g

Fat: 13 g (8 g saturated)

Cholesterol: 0 mg

Potassium: 153 mg

Phosphorus: 55 mg

Calcium: 13 mg

Sodium: 5 mg

Iron: 1 mg

CHOCOLATE CHIP MERINGUE CLOUDS p. 268
(Serving size: 1 meringue)

Calories: 67 kcal

Carbs: 12 g (10 g sugar, 0 g of fiber)

Protein: 1 g

Fat: 2 g (1 g saturated)

Cholesterol: 0 mg

Potassium: 32 mg

Phosphorus: 12 mg

Calcium: 3 mg

Sodium: 15 mg

Iron: 1 mg

CHOCOLATE CHUNK CRANBERRY COOKIES p. 264
(Serving size: 1 large cookie)

Calories: 298 kcal

Carbs: 43 g (32 g sugar, 2 g of fiber)

Protein: 3 g

Fat: 14 g (4 g saturated)

Cholesterol: 21 mg

Potassium: 93 mg

Phosphorus: 43 mg

Calcium: 19 mg

Sodium: 95 mg

Iron: 1 mg

COCONUT ROCKY ROAD BARK p. 278
Calories: 522 kcal
Carbs: 48 g (35 g sugar, 8 g of fiber)
Protein: 9 g
Fat: 38 g (18 g saturated)
Cholesterol: 0 mg
Potassium: 447 mg
Phosphorus: 219 mg
Calcium: 89 mg
Sodium: 19 mg
Iron: 3 mg

CRANBERRY-CORNFLAKE BISCOTTI p. 270
(Serving size: 1 biscotto)
Calories: 134 kcal
Carbs: 18 g (11 g sugar, 1 g of fiber)
Protein: 1 g
Fat: 7 g (1 g saturated)
Cholesterol: 10 mg
Potassium: 14 mg
Phosphorus: 19 mg
Calcium: 19 mg
Sodium: 62 mg
Iron: 1 mg

FLOURLESS FUDGY-WUDGY COOKIES p. 266
(Serving size: 1 cookie)
Calories: 76 kcal
Carbs: 14 g (13 g sugar, 1 g of fiber)
Protein: 1 g
Fat: 2 g (1 g saturated)
Cholesterol: 1 mg
Potassium: 65 mg
Phosphorus: 31 mg
Calcium: 15 mg
Sodium: 19 mg
Iron: 0 mg

FUDGY PRETZEL BROWNIES p. 276
(Serving size: 1 brownie)
Calories: 217 kcal
Carbs: 28 g (17 g sugar, 1 g of fiber)
Protein: 3 g
Fat: 12 g (2 g saturated)
Cholesterol: 23 mg
Potassium: 97 mg
Phosphorus: 51 mg
Calcium: 23 mg
Sodium: 101 mg
Iron: 1 mg

THE GREEN FRUIT SALAD p. 288
Calories: 135 kcal
Carbs: 34 g (27 g sugar, 4 g of fiber)
Protein: 1 g
Fat: 0 g (0 g saturated)
Cholesterol: 0 mg
Potassium: 426 mg
Phosphorus: 37 mg
Calcium: 24 mg
Sodium: 14 mg
Iron: 1 mg

PISTACHIO BISCOTTI p. 272
(Serving size: 1 biscotto)
Calories: 121 kcal
Carbs: 15 g (9 g sugar, 1 g of fiber)
Protein: 2 g
Fat: 7 g (2 g saturated)
Cholesterol: 10 mg
Potassium: 62 mg
Phosphorus: 35 mg
Calcium: 18 mg
Sodium: 32 mg
Iron: 1 mg

POMEGRANATE ALMOND CHOCOLATE BARK p. 278
Calories: 336 kcal
Carbs: 39 g (31 g sugar, 6 g of fiber)
Protein: 5 g
Fat: 22 g (9 g saturated)
Cholesterol: 0 mg
Potassium: 333 mg
Phosphorus: 139 mg
Calcium: 54 mg
Sodium: 6 mg
Iron: 2 mg

RAINBOW PRETZELS p. 286
(Serving size: 1 pretzel)
Calories: 226 kcal
Carbs: 40 g (25 g sugar, 1 g of fiber)
Protein: 2 g
Fat: 8 g (5 g saturated)
Cholesterol: 0 mg
Potassium: 87 mg
Phosphorus: 34 mg
Calcium: 8 mg
Sodium: 154 mg
Iron: 1 mg

TRAIL MIX CHOCOLATE BARK p. 279
Calories: 490 kcal
Carbs: 54 g (42 g sugar, 7 g of fiber)
Protein: 10 g
Fat: 31 g (42 g saturated)
Cholesterol: 0 mg
Potassium: 390 mg
Phosphorus: 434 mg
Calcium: 38 mg
Sodium: 9 mg
Iron: 3 mg

ULTIMATE CHOCOLATE CHIP COOKIES p. 260
(serving: 1 cookie)
Calories: 416 kcal
Carbs: 52 g (36 g sugar, 2 g of fiber)
Protein: 4 g
Fat: 24 g (7 g saturated)
Cholesterol: 25 mg
Potassium: 144 mg
Phosphorus: 74 mg
Calcium: 42 mg
Sodium: 247 mg
Iron: 2 mg

WHITE CHOCOLATE CHIP & DRIED APRICOT COOKIES p. 262
(Serving size: 1 cookie)
Calories: 310 kcal
Carbs: 41 g (28 g sugar, 2 g of fiber)
Protein: 4 g
Fat: 15 g (4 g saturated)
Cholesterol: 19 mg
Potassium: 193 mg
Phosphorus: 49 mg
Calcium: 50 mg
Sodium: 24 mg
Iron: 1

WHITE CHOCOLATE POPCORN CLUSTERS p. 284
Calories: 298 kcal
Carbs: 50 g (37 g sugar, 5 g of fiber)
Protein: 3 g
Fat: 13 g (8 g saturated)
Cholesterol: 0 mg
Potassium: 190 mg
Phosphorus: 87 mg
Calcium: 14 mg
Sodium: 5 mg
Iron: 2 mg

WHITE CHOCOLATE PRETZEL BARK p. 279
Calories: 523 kcal
Carbs: 71 g (50 g sugar, 4 g of fiber)
Protein: 6 g
Fat: 28 g (16 g saturated)
Cholesterol: 8 mg
Potassium: 350 mg
Phosphorus: 159 mg
Calcium: 96 mg
Sodium: 281 mg
Iron: 3 mg

CAKES

ALMOND-CRUSTED CHOCOLATE TART p. 310
Calories: 600 kcal
Carbs: 46 g (35 g sugar, 7 g of fiber)
Protein: 11 g
Fat: 46 g (15 g saturated)
Cholesterol: 24 mg
Potassium: 306 mg
Phosphorus: 142 mg
Calcium: 132 mg
Sodium: 14 mg
Iron: 3 mg

APPLE CINNAMON CAKE p. 292
Calories: 457 kcal
Carbs: 65 g (39 g sugar, 3 g of fiber)
Protein: 5 g
Fat: 21 g (3 g saturated)
Cholesterol: 62 mg
Potassium: 139 mg
Phosphorus: 95 mg
Calcium: 98 mg
Sodium: 193 mg
Iron: 2 mg

BANANA CHOCOLATE CHIP CAKE p. 294
Calories: 398 kcal
Carbs: 59 g (35 g sugar, 2 g of fiber)
Protein: 5 g
Fat: 18 g (5 g saturated)
Cholesterol: 37 mg
Potassium: 252 mg
Phosphorus: 86 mg
Calcium: 63 mg
Sodium: 196 mg
Iron: 2 mg

BLUEBERRY FLAN p. 312
Calories: 363 kcal
Carbs: 58 g (32 g sugar, 4 g of fiber)
Protein: 3 g
Fat: 15 g (2 g saturated)
Cholesterol: 0 mg
Potassium: 119 mg
Phosphorus: 42 mg
Calcium: 14 mg
Sodium: 2 mg
Iron: 2 mg

CARROT CAKE WITH COCONUT TOPPING p. 296
(Values for cake without topping)
Calories: 789 kcal
Carbs: 72 g (48 g sugar, 3g of fiber)
Protein: 8 g
Fat: 54 g (16 g saturated)
Cholesterol: 126 mg
Potassium: 258 mg
Phosphorus: 151 mg
Calcium: 133 mg
Sodium: 562 mg
Iron: 2 mg

(Values for topping)
Calories: 244 kcal
Carbs: 18 g (16 g sugar, 1 g of fiber)
Protein: 3 g
Fat: 18 g (11 g saturated)
Cholesterol: 51 mg
Potassium: 96 mg
Phosphorus: 58 mg
Calcium: 46 mg
Sodium: 194 mg
Iron: 0 mg

CHOCOLATE CHIP BERRY CAKE p. 304
Calories: 498 kcal
Carbs: 70 g (36 g sugar, 3 g of fiber)
Protein: 7 g
Fat: 23 g (5 g saturated)
Cholesterol: 47 mg
Potassium: 170 mg
Phosphorus: 116 mg
Calcium: 94 mg
Sodium: 294 mg
Iron: 3 mg

COOKIE CAKE p. 306
Calories- 602
Carbs- 74 (45 g sugar, 2 g fiber)
Protein- 6 g
Fat- 34 g (7 g saturated)
Cholesterol- 47 g
Potassium- 195 mg
Phosphorus- 82 mg
Calcium- 41 mg
Sodium- 309 mg
Iron- 3 mg

CRANBERRY-BLUEBERRY CRUMBLE p. 314
Calories: 227 kcal
Carbs: 41 g (23 g sugar, 5 g of fiber)
Protein: 2 g
Fat: 7 g (1 g saturated)
Cholesterol: 0 mg
Potassium: 137 mg
Phosphorus: 29 mg
Calcium: 28 mg
Sodium: 6 mg
Iron: 1 mg

DOUBLE-GLAZED MARBLE CAKE p. 302
Calories: 591 kcal
Carbs: 86 g (95 g sugar, 2 g of fiber)
Protein: 6 g
Fat: 27 g (4 g saturated)
Cholesterol: 47 mg
Potassium: 118 mg
Phosphorus: 90 mg
Calcium: 44 mg
Sodium: 233 mg
Iron: 2 mg

FLOURLESS CHOCOLATE MOUSSE CAKE p. 298
Calories: 319 kcal
Carbs: 33 g (31 g sugar, 1 g of fiber)
Protein: 5 g
Fat: 20 g (7 g saturated)
Cholesterol: 124 mg
Potassium: 135 mg
Phosphorus: 90 mg
Calcium: 25 mg
Sodium: 44 mg
Iron: 1 mg

HEAVENLY HALVAH CHEESECAKE p. 316
Calories: 634 kcal
Carbs: 52 g (44 g sugar, 1 g of fiber)
Protein: 10 g
Fat: 44 g (23 g saturated)
Cholesterol: 191 mg
Potassium: 207 mg
Phosphorus: 201 mg
Calcium: 116 mg
Sodium: 420 mg
Iron: 1 mg

POMEGRANATE-GLAZED HONEY CAKE p. 308
Calories: 347 kcal
Carbs: 78 g (55 g sugar, 1 g of fiber)
Protein: 5 g
Fat: 3 g (1 g saturated)
Cholesterol: 47 mg
Potassium: 89 mg
Phosphorus: 72 mg
Calcium: 61 mg
Sodium: 204 mg
Iron: 2 mg

ROCKY ROAD BROWNIE CAKE p. 300
Calories: 439 kcal
Carbs: 61 g (41 g sugar, 2 g of fiber)
Protein: 4 g
Fat: 23 g (4 g saturated)
Cholesterol: 62 mg
Potassium: 130 mg
Phosphorus: 78 mg
Calcium: 18 mg
Sodium: 33 mg
Iron: 1 mg

"All of our favorites, for the everyday to the Holidays"

Index

Thank You

TO MY RECIPE TESTERS: ROSALIE ANTMAN, NENITA AQUINO, ROBYN BARNETT, CINDY BEER, MELISSA BERGER, CHAYALA BISTRICER, BRENDA BORZYKOWSKI, ELISE BRADT, MIRIAM BURKE, FERNE COHEN, AHUVA EDELL, FELICE FLEGG, MONA FRANK, SARAH GAL, RENEE GLASS, NAOMI GLUSTEIN, RIVKA GROSSMAN, RITA GROSS, PENNY GUTFREUND, LEORA GRUNBAUM, SHOSHANA HAHN, EMILY HERSHTAL, ALI ISAKOW, MARSHA JOHNSTON, ISSAC KAPLAN, CHANI KAPLAN, YAEL KATZMAN, JENNIFER KNIGHT, VITA KOLODNY, FRANCES KRAFT, PAM KUHL, ILANA LEVOVSKI, EVE LIPSYC, RESA LITWACK, EDEN LITWACK, MARLA MARCUS, HELENE MEDJUCK, RENA NEUFELD, LAUREN NUSSBAUM, BRENDA PERLMUTTER, JUDY POLLICK, PENINA POPPER, RACHELI RAPP, CAROL ROSENSTOCK, SHELAH SALTZMAN, SHOSHANA SCHACHTER, BONNY SILVER, SHERRI SILVER, SUSAN SILVERMAN, TALI SIMON, SHAYNA TRAIN, SOPHIA SPIRO, BEVERLEE SWAYZE, CHANTAL ULMER, DORI WEISS, JULI WEINTRAUB, ALYSSA WIESEL, JUDITH WEXLER, ATARA YUNGER, and DALIA YUNGER. Thank you for your help in making this cookbook a reality. It's because of all of you that I was able to experiment and create spectacular recipes, and it's because of you that I can now share them with the world. Your invaluable support and feedback have allowed me to move confidently ahead. Thank you again, and eat well!

And to HELENE MEDJUCK: An extra thank-you for all your extra help and support.